Coldwater Fish in Aquaria and Garden Ponds

Roy Pinks

Illustrations by Rex Nicholls

John Bartholomew & Son Limited
Edinburgh

First published in Great Britain 1981 by
John Bartholomew & Son Limited,
12 Duncan Street, Edinburgh, EH9 1TA.

© John Bartholomew & Son Limited, 1981

ISBN 0 7028 8360 3

British Library Cataloguing in Publication Data
Pinks, Roy
    Coldwater fish in aquaria and garden ponds
    1. Aquarium fishes
    2. Water gardens
    I. Title
    639'.34   SF457

Printed in Great Britain by
John Bartholomew & Son Limited, Edinburgh

Contents

1 Fish in an aquarium become very tame

Introduction

This book is intended as an introductory guide to the culture of coldwater fish in fresh water. It is not an instruction manual. The distinction is most important. The behaviour of fish is so unpredictable that it is not possible to make rigid rules as to their care and treatment. Even within species, individuals can vary noticeably in terms of both appearance and behaviour, and we should take nothing for granted. Yet, their unpredictability is not so great that their management is unduly difficult or beyond our physical or financial means. The truth of the matter is that most living creatures display tendencies, rather than blind and automatic reactions, to what happens around them.

If we are to manage them successfully we must try to find out just how flexible they really are under the varying sets of conditions to which they may be subjected. We constantly come across instances of successful fishkeeping under circumstances incredibly at odds with our own experience, and we must therefore bear in mind that we still do not know all the answers. There are nevertheless sound general guidelines which will help the beginner on his way, and this book aims to cover these in some detail.

In recent years more and more people have taken up fishkeeping in one form or another, and this trend seems likely to increase as world events, economic pressures and environmental shortcomings drive individuals to seek solace and inspiration from the beauty of living things. Coldwater fishkeeping seems to have an especially bright future as it does not depend upon expensive electricity to support it, and it is not affected by strikes and similar privations.

Apart from the decorative tank in the home and the equally attractive pond in the garden, installations are found in many other circumstances. The invalid finds companionship, the patient in the waiting room finds distraction from the aching tooth, and the corporation president finds comfort after his investments have slipped yet again. The specialist finds an absorbing and possibly mildly profitable sideline by breeding and selling surplus specimen fish, and the dweller in high rise flats can find compensation for the garden he will never have. All these applications of a fascinating hobby are immensely rewarding and, as will become evident, both the maintenance cost and the effort required are quite low by comparison with many other pastimes.

There is however one important underlying principle which must apply to all who have anything to do with living things. We must recognize the dignity which all creatures possess, and we must respect it for as long as we have them in our charge.

2 Common (foreground) and fancy goldfish

Planning and General Management

Before you begin to acquire tanks and fish and to dig holes in the lawn, it is important that you take pencil and paper and make plans of what you have in mind. More often than not the newcomer to the hobby sets out with the determination to confine his interests to a single tank, but later expands his installation to match a growing enthusiasm. If this is carried out haphazardly, disappointment and unnecessary expense are almost inevitable. Initial planning should take the form of a mental picture of how future additions will relate to furnishings, the home in general, and the garden. Some rough sketches and costings should then be attempted and discussed with those likely to be affected. If the lady of the house is consulted she may well point out that the style of the proposed cabinet for the tanks will clash badly with the existing furniture, adding that if this job is combined with the construction of the new kitchen cupboards, the materials can be ordered in bulk, and will prove cheaper in the long run. More ambitious undertakings, like the building of a fish house, may require planning permission from the local authority, and as neighbours may have a voice in this matter, discussions with them at an early stage will prove useful as well as politic.

From the purely constructional and economic point of view it is preferable to build a lot, rather than a little, if it seems likely that your hobby will grow. The best example of this is the cabinet capable of housing several tanks in a living room. This has to look attractive and professional and is best completed as a single job. If you simply add bits as you need them, you may not notice the joins and the variations in shade of wood or paint, but your visitors certainly will.

The most suitable spot for a garden pond is often a difficult choice, and it is best to prepare several mock-ups, using rope or string and long canes, to indicate on the ground where the excavations will be. These should be viewed from a number of angles before the first sod is cut. This is particularly important to the would-be breeder who intends building a number of small ponds for spawning and rearing. These are usually functional and rather stark, but can be made unobtrusive with a little imagination. Poor planning here could lead to some depreciation in the value of house property, as few prospective purchasers are likely to be attracted by ugly fishponds.

Much successful fishkeeping depends on having patience at the right times. There are two main stages at which this is necessary. The first, as emphasized above, is at the planning stage. The way in which planning is carried out depends upon your taste and the size of your proposed installation: the vital thing is that a plan, however sketchy, does emerge. The other stage at which restraint must be exercised is when plantings in aquarium and pond are being carried out. The reader is asked to accept that there are no such things as successful 'instant' aquaria or 'instant' ponds. They simply do not exist.

Some basic principles

All fishkeeping can be condensed into a few words. If you give a fish enough oxygen and light it will live. If you give it enough food it will survive. If you give it enough room it will thrive, and if you give it the right companions it will breed.

The most important of these rules is the first — that enough oxygen be provided for the fish to carry out its normal functions. This is dealt with in detail in the section on aeration. Meanwhile it may be said that our main job in managing an aquarium or pond is to increase the overall availability of oxygen and to reduce the counter-balancing factors.

The first thing to aim for is planned under-stocking. If your tank will normally accommodate, say, 12in (30cm) length of fish, only stock it with about half that amount. The calculation is usually based on an allowance of 20 sq in (130 sq cm) of water surface area to every 1in (2.5cm) of fish, excluding the tail. In the case of ponds allow a significantly greater margin to cope with an accelerated growth rate and with breeding. With a newly established pond it is probably better to introduce no more than a pair or a trio of breeding specimens. They will usually demonstrate their appreciation of ideal conditions by spawning prolifically during their first season.

Selective planting will also help to prevent imbalances, especially if allowed enough time to consolidate before fish are introduced. In the initial seasoning period of any body of water there is fierce competition between the higher plants, which we introduce, and the millions of minute plant organisms, collectively called algae, which exist in the water. The higher plants will do quite well in restricted light, but algae multiply rapidly in the higher ranges of illumination, and the water often turns green soon after the tank or the pond has been set up. Many owners panic at this point and pour in some form of algae killer recommended at the local pet store. Nothing could be worse, since algicides destroy plants too, and they join the dying algae on the tank or pond bed and begin to rot. This process produces carbon dioxide and other toxic chemicals which will harm or kill the fish. The best way to cure green water is to increase the amount of shade, perhaps by reducing tank lighting or by increasing the number of floating plants in the pond. If fish are not yet present, the introduction of a small quantity of *daphnia* (water fleas) will bring about a return to crystal clear conditions, and will form a splendid introductory meal for the fish when they eventually arrive in their new home.

Just as too many fish will reduce the oxygen level below survival point, excesses of food or of plants can have equally serious consequences. Assuming that you feed fish with dry food and allow them the right quantity, which is as much as they can dispose of within about five minutes, a little of this will sink to the bottom where it will either be snapped up later or worked upon by bacteria. Millions of these invisible workers are usually congregated in the gravel, on rocks and similar surfaces. When excesses of decaying material begin to accumulate the oxygen content of the water drops and the beneficial bacteria are replaced by anaerobic bacteria (those which do not require oxygen for survival). The resultant process culminates in what we recognize as pollution. There is often clouding of the water, a disgusting smell, and, in advanced cases, the presence of dead fish. These processes may be quite local, as in the area under a feeding ring, which in many tanks appears as a black patch, indicating that anaerobic bacteria are present. If conditions in such a tank begin to deteriorate to the point at which the fish are only just holding their own, it takes very little to trigger off a collapse.

Excesses of plant life can also contribute to oxygen deficiency, and this is because plants expire carbon dioxide at night. In the average tank correct stocking and aeration usually prevent dangerous imbalance, and much the same applies to ponds, where the fish to surface area ratio is fairly low. However, conditions can change rapidly and the early morning period can prove stressful to the oxygen-greedy fish like orfe and rudd, whilst goldfish and sluggish species, such as tench, are not usually affected.

This is exemplified by the heavy losses of orfe and the like during periods of thundery or heavy weather conditions, when the fish may be seen rolling on their sides and gasping for air. Immediate help can be given by the violent addition of water straight from the garden hose, followed by a partial water change and then a topping up. Yet all too often the gills of the fish have been permanently damaged by the temporary deficiency of oxygen and the victims perish. This is as strong an argument as I know for stocking at a quarter or less of the recommended figure.

Winter conditions in a pond produce similar dangers when the water surface is frozen over. If there is an excess of decaying matter in the pond, fatalities are almost bound to occur even though 'blow holes' are made in the ice to allow the escape of toxic gases.

The reader will by now appreciate that if nature is allowed a completely free hand the tank and the pond will at some stage get out of our control. To prevent this we need to carry out regular maintenance and inspection routines. These are not very onerous, but they are central to successful management, and we must try to work out a system whereby we are reminded of what to do, and when. Faulty management often stems from the mistaken notion that the performance of one tank containing a goldfish will be the same as that from another similarly sized tank containing a similar goldfish. Many aquarists have found to their cost that variations of local conditions often cause unexpected results from what are apparently identical aquaria situated within a few inches of one another. The same applies to ponds, and no two require quite the same treatment, so you should handle each on its own merits if you are to achieve the best results. The factors which influence conditions are such things as light or shade, the fact that one pond receives a leaf fall from a tree, whilst another does not, or that the baby has poured some orangeade into one tank but not another. You may not have noticed these things happening, so look around for unusual causes if something goes wrong.

The capture of fish can be quite a nightmare, but cunning is better than brute force. In a tank two nets should be used to coax the fish into a position from which it can be netted calmly; spirited chases are likely to result in loss of scales, which allow infections to take a hold. Serious dislocation of the plantings also occurs if the tank is a decorative one. In a pond everything depends on its configuration, and in larger ones individual fish can usually only be caught by draining. Bottle traps containing worms may be tried, and sometimes it is possible to lay fine netting on a pond shelf, feed the fish above it, and then whisk it out. This, though, is not selective, nor is it very efficient. A method often adopted is to shine a bright torch light on the fish after dark and to slip a net under them while they are momentarily dazzled — this very often works. In ponds it is wise to provide a wide and shallow shelf, as fish resting there at night, in the warmer water, do not immediately dive to the depths, thus eluding capture.

Safety and security are matters which must also concern the fish-keeper today. Electrical safety may be achieved by disconnecting all mains leads when servicing tanks or pond equipment (even low voltage), and regular examination should be made of all wiring, connectors and distribution points. Fish houses must be correctly wired, taking account of the need to keep wires away from visitors, and of the possible dangers arising from condensation. They should also be fitted with mortice locks to deter thieves and vandals; an electronic alarm should also be considered. The risks to children can be reduced by encircling the pond with some form of netting or by building it with a raised wall: many fatalities arising from drowning could have been prevented by such simple precautions. If it is essential to work on any electrically live installation, work with one hand and keep the other in your pocket.

As fish and plants are becoming increasingly expensive it is sensible to attempt to maintain your supplies from existing stock, and the pondkeeper in particular has the annual worry of just how an exceptionally severe winter might trim his resources. It will therefore pay him to set aside a tank, under cover, in which surplus fish and plants from the pond can be overwintered. In the event of severe losses there would be a supply of acclimatized stock ready for the warmer days of the new season. If the winter turns out to be kinder than expected, there would be some welcome presents for friends.

Management is not merely a series of 'Do's and Don'ts', neatly numbered and docketed. On the contrary, it is more often the instinctive application of one's experience to a given situation, and it sometimes fails to work because the conditions have been misread. The sensible fishkeeper will pick up all manner of information which comes his way — from books, the aquatic press and from discussion with members of the local club. A potent source of useful information is a five year diary, in which all significant events should be recorded, together with weather conditions and similar items of interest. Dates of acquisition of fish, of spawning and hatching, and when the first ice appeared on the pool do not seem very vital in the first year, but when there is a record of such data over several years, consultation of the diary will give valuable pointers as to what jobs need to be tackled during the next week or so in your locality. Local librarians are very helpful people and, if you need books for further guidance or research, you will find their professional approach to your requirements will be both sympathetic and efficient.

Acquiring Pond and Aquarium Fish

I will define coldwater fish as those which do not require artificial heating to maintain them in health in either tank or pond in this country. This is not quite right, as there are great variations in climate between extreme north and south, but it will do for all practical purposes.

Long before you buy a single specimen you should have decided why you want to keep fish, and plan the nature of your purchases accordingly. The student will have a fairly clear idea of his aims, but the general fishkeeper should try to decide whether he wants them for the pure interest they bring, for decoration, or for breeding. Perhaps there is a combination of all three. These varied motives will often determine what is obtained, where to get it, and what quality of stock is required.

Let us attempt a few subdivisions. The first category comprises the *cultivated* species, in which the Goldfish and Koi are included. These do not breed true to type. Obviously, the second category will be the *wild* or *natural* species, which do breed true to type and which in many cases may be captured from ponds and other waters in this country. The second subdivision I would make puts fish under the headings of *compatible* species and those which are *incompatible*. The former covers species which are ideal for mixed collections. Incompatible fish are those which are either positively harmful to peaceful species, like perch, or which do so much better in quarters dedicated to their use, that they are best kept on their own, and the increasingly popular Koi features here. A third subdivision would be those species best kept in a *pond*, as compared with those which are best displayed in the unheated *aquarium*. In the former class, Koi would again feature, and the Stickleback would be a firm contender for the second. Try to place the fish which you may be considering into these slots: later I will elaborate on this in relation to individual species. Other criteria may occur to the reader and should be applied to all candidates before purchase.

When you have considered your preferences and selected the most likely starters for your pond or aquarium, think about their likely source of supply. Although it will often be the local dealer, the specialist breeder will prove more satisfactory if you aim to breed quality fish. You will sometimes get what you need from friends, but this often consists of rejected specimens which may disappoint. Finally, you may be able to catch your own fish. Scorn is often directed at the taking of fish from the wild, on the grounds that they are disease-ridden. However, many species simply cannot be obtained by any other means, and they are often found to be more healthy than many imports of fancy species, an increasing proportion of which have exhibited serious disease symptoms during recent years. Hence the value and integrity of home-bred coldwater fish cannot be too strongly emphasized. Fish caught by hook and line will often survive if the mouth damage is not too severe, and they should then be quarantined in water containing acriflavine. Wild fish can sometimes be taken from the shallows of local waters. Swift random plunges with a stout long-handled net will often yield surprisingly good results, but do take care that there are no licensing restrictions!

The aquatic press always contains a good selection of possible suppliers, and price lists should be studied with some care. It is advisable to buy the smallest fish available, and to grow them on to fit the tank or pond, rather than to acquire those tempting giant specimens in the hope that they will fit in. The latter may have already outgrown the scale of accommodation you are able to offer, and will always be under some form of stress in having to exist in less than optimum conditions. This, at least, is the best advice for the beginner, who will take some pleasure in watching small fish put on size over several seasons. The experienced fish-keeper will indeed buy large specimens for breeding, but he will first have made sure that the environment he is offering will accommodate them successfully.

Although most suppliers will send fish by rail or other carrier, it

14

is better to collect what you need yourself. If you have a large order, do avoid just turning up, hoping that you can depart half an hour later with every item complete. It is as well to contact the specialist beforehand to make sure that what you want is available, and that he will be open for business when you arrive. Many firms do not begin netting until much later in the year than some customers realize, and in the middle of a summer heatwave they will rightly decline to sell species like orfe, which may suffer severely during long journeys.

Whatever route your fish take to reach your premises, they must be given a long period in quarantine. A suitable container for this purpose is a plastic lined air transit fish box, which should be placed in a cool and shady spot and covered in such a way that the fish receive plenty of air but cannot jump out. A sterilizing agent may be placed in the water, but is not essential, and many aquarists prefer to defer the addition of chemicals of any sort until disease is positively identified. A fortnight's seclusion is about right, and longer is better still. To maintain the fish in good health during this period, food should comprise *daphnia* and chopped whiteworm or earthworm, but this must not be fed to excess. Special precautions are necessary when buying coldwater fish from local dealers, and on no account should they be placed directly outdoors unless the weather is warm. This is because most coldwater fish from shops are kept in a temperature well above that prevailing in the garden pond, and if the weather is on the cold side an acclimatization process must be carried out.

Disease is most unlikely to attack sound coldwater stock which has been placed in a favourable environment. Even so, there is a high level of most virulent disease amongst imports, and the rule must be that no fish whatever should be bought from a dealer's tank in which there is evidence of disease, especially that in which large open reddish ulcers appear on the body of the fish. If in doubt it is best to take an experienced aquarist with you before buying. The following are a few points to watch for. The fish should be swimming on an even keel and not rolling in any way. Thin bellies and pinched-looking bodies should be avoided, and scales should all be present. All fins should be glistening and erect, and the fish too should look glowing, with bright and clear eyes. Watch the breathing rate and reject any specimens which seem to have a higher count than the others in the tank. Any tufts of white fungus or raised white spots on the body certainly indicate disease. Frayed and dull fins point to poor condition, and shortened tails usually lead to death. Fish which look busy, and which are doing something purposeful in a crowded tank, are likely to be better value than those which sit in mid-water looking aimless and rocking gently from side to side. Scales projecting from the body may indicate dropsy, from which fish seldom recover, or some physical injury, itself an inlet for disease.

3 Fin rot and fungus

Some Diseases and their Treatment

In some cases of ill health the fish will make it clear to you that they are in distress, but with certain ailments they are more passive, so a careful watch should be kept on the condition of your fish at all times. Clamped fins, lowered dorsals in particular, are immediate warnings, and every suspect fish should be netted and placed in a hospital tank.

The following group of complaints comprises some of those in which the fish signals that something is wrong, usually by rubbing the afflicted part on a rock or leaf, and sometimes by an increased rate of breathing:

Whitespot, or *Ichthyopthirius,* is not very common with coldwater fish, but can be fatal. The victim continually flicks its body against some obstruction and displays scores of tiny white raised spots on its body and fins. The parasite progresses through a cycle in which the fish becomes increasingly spotted, and unless the organisms are killed the fish will die of general weakness. They exist both on the fish and in its environment, and treatments, which may have to be repeated, usually attack this parasite when it is external to the fish. Recent medications claim to kill it when it is affixed to the fish, and they often clear up the trouble within a day or so. Treatments include Chloramine T, Methylene Blue, Quinine hydrochloride, and Malachite Green, the last of which is particularly successful.

Gill flukes cause the fish to rub their gill plates against hard surfaces, and increased respiration is an accompanying symptom. Methylene Blue or Acriflavine may be added to the tank water or, alternatively, a few seconds' bath in weak Dettol (15ml to 4.5 litres of water) should prove effective.

Anchor worms are external parasites, appearing as small white nodules on the body of the fish, from which the worm protrudes. A salt bath (25g to 4.5 litres) is sometimes effective, but more drastic treatment, such as dabbing with cotton wool dipped in bleach, weak Dettol or ammonia, may become necessary.

Costia and other small skin parasites are barely visible, but discomfort is obvious, and a quick bath in weak Dettol will again help. Mercurochrome is an alternative.

Fish louse (Argulus) is a flat, rounded, jelly-like bloodsucker which digs into the flesh of the fish, and which can be removed with forceps, though I do not recommend this with small specimens as the shock often kills the victim as well. Dab the louse with cotton wool soaked in weak Dettol or turpentine, or try a mercurochrome bath. When the parasite has been removed, ensure that the wound is protected until healed, by keeping the fish in water containing a little acriflavine. Fish do not always display distress symptoms with this unpleasant customer, but they become very weak and can become grossly infested.

Swim bladder trouble may be diagnosed from loss of balance, erratic and aimless swimming, and desperate paddling with the pectoral fins. It is physiological and complete cures rarely occur. A general upgrading of food and conditions, including temperature, sometimes improves matters.

In the following conditions the fish do not behave markedly differently from usual, but there are physical manifestations of disease.

Fungus is a very common condition, in which white or grey tufts like cotton wool appear on the body of the fish. It can be readily treated by keeping the fish in salt water — 1oz to 1 gallon (25g to 4.5 litres), or by the use of a medication including phenoxethol.

Fin rot and *fin congestion* can sometimes be improved by better food, warmer conditions and a water change, but phenoxethol or acriflavine may be needed in some cases. A salt treatment, as recommended above, may also be tried.

Mouth rot is a serious bacterial condition which often proves fatal, and the more drastic treatments like dilute Dettol or phenoxethol will need to be used.

I have not attempted, excepting in the case of household cures like salt, to recommend dosages. The chemicals mentioned are intended to guide you to the right type of medicine offered by your supplier, who will often be able to help you if you are unsure of your own diagnosis. When using medicines always relate the dose to the size of the fish, which should be removed from the tank if it shows signs of distress.

Pests

There are numerous pests like water boatmen, the larvae of water beetles, nymphs of dragonflies, and the jelly-like polyp, *Hydra,* which are usually more of a worry to the pondkeeper than the aquarist. Since they usually only attack and feed on small fish, thus thinning them out, many fishkeepers simply ignore them. If you wish to preserve as many of your young fish as possible, most of these harmful creatures can be netted and destroyed. *Hydra* are extremely persistent and can only be eliminated by taking down the tank or emptying the pond and sterilizing their contents.

Killing fish

Fish which reach a state of obviously irreversible distress should be put out of their agony. The swiftest way is to put the fish in a plastic bag and to dash this hard against a concrete path several times. It is unpleasant, but you have an obligation to limit suffering. The bag and contents should then be burnt.

Handling fish

Fish sometimes have to be handled during medication, and this must invariably be done with wet hands or a wet soft cloth. Dry material will remove scales and pave the way to further infection. Fish which have jumped out of their containers should never be written off just because they look dead. Return them to their normal water: in many cases there will be the most surprising recoveries once the dust and fluff have washed off.

Limitations in treatment

Treatment of fish disease is comparatively simple in the aquarium, from which the afflicted fish may be netted without great difficulty, but the pond is a different matter, and in situ medication is either downright impossible or prohibitively expensive. The breeder is most affected if disease strikes one of his ponds, and he may have to decide to drain it and treat the fish in small groups, temporarily accommodated in external containers. The more general fishkeeper may have to accept the fact that treatment is beyond his capability, and will let nature take its course. It is seldom that all the fish succumb to odd outbreaks of disease in a pond, and even if there are heavy losses, there is some consolation that the survivors may have developed a form of immunity.

It should also be said that for most maladies there are several possible treatments. Success depends on the size and the physical state of the fish at the time of treatment; unfortunately, the cure is often as fatal as the disease, and under-dosing is recommended, as the strength can be increased if necessary. Failure to cure a fish exhibiting certain symptoms is not always due to the ineffectiveness of a medicine. The fish may have died from an invisible cause, whilst a secondary, visible, condition developed, far too late to alert the aquarist to the true state of affairs. Beware of false symptoms too. Sometimes there is a milky, slimy, fungus-like exudation on fish, notably the fancy goldfish, often occurring after the winter rest. This is nothing to worry about and it usually disappears as the season unfolds. With some specimens, especially lionhead and oranda goldfish in aquaria, this persists, but there are no ill effects. White tubercles often appear on the gill plates of male goldfish in the breeding season, and these should not be confused with whitespot, which is smaller and more widely distributed.

Antibiotics

Recent research indicates growing success in the treatment of ailments like fin and body rot ('hole in the body disease') with broad spectrum antibiotics, of which Terramycin is an example. These are only available on prescription, and your local veterinary surgeon will be able to help if you wish to apply this sort of treatment. Medication is best applied in a separate aquarium, from which the sick fish can be removed if it shows signs of undue distress.

The Aquarium

The main installation

Some years ago it was usual to speak of tanks in terms of standard sizes, and of construction based on metal or wooden frameworks, on one-piece plastic mouldings, and on metal frames coated with protective plastic layers. Whilst these are still freely available, the newer technique of making all-glass tanks by using a sealant to join the panels of glass together has really come to stay. The process is not difficult for the average handyman. In the course of construction the silicone which occurs naturally in glass is automatically welded with that in the sealant, and if the work is properly done, a one-piece tank is created. Scepticism that this type of tank would come apart after a time has been allayed by a high measure of success, and the few bursts which have occurred have been due either to faulty workmanship or failure to incorporate adequate bracing elements in very large tanks. This form of construction enables us to order the exact size required for a particular situation, and imparts a tailor-made look to even the most modest installation.

Mock wrought-iron stands have been used to house aquaria for many years, but there has recently been a shift in preference to purpose-built cabinets incorporating not only the tanks but also storage space for food and equipment. They look much better as items of furniture and also help to conceal the air lines, wires and similar distractions which normally festoon the conventional stand. Safety is another by-product of this approach, because the enquiring fingers of small children can be excluded completely from the tank top, which is the main danger area. You are therefore now in a position to ask your dealer to make you an all-glass tank to your own specification. This can include decorative end panels if you wish, and you should make sure that he will also provide inlets for air lines, a support for the cover glass (which is ideally formed by sliding panels), and a support for the hood which houses the lighting arrangements. Consider the proportions of the tank before you finalize the order, always allowing maximum provision for surface area of water, and increase the depth to match increases in length.

In planning the externals of your tank you should give some thought to the possible value of allowing some space adjoining the back and sides for the accommodation of containers for plants, moss, rocks, cork bark, etc., which give an impression of greater depth of scenery, and are often the saviour of the aquarist who simply cannot cope with plants because either his fish eat them or they succumb to algae. It requires tasteful arrangement however for such ancillary decoration to prove a success. An indoor installation can eventually take up a lot of room, and in the process it can become extremely heavy because of a growing volume of water in use. It may therefore be as well to take professional advice as to stresses and strains on the structure of the house or flat, as any accidents arising from this source can be dangerous as well as extremely costly.

When siting tanks you should avoid direct sunlight as this encourages the growth of algae, which may prove difficult to control. If anything, plan for a shadier rather than a sunnier spot, because you can always make use of artificial lighting and this will avoid having to diminish the cheering effects of sunlight elsewhere in the room. Assuming also the likelihood that your interests will grow, do make sure that you really have got room for further tanks. A sound seating must be provided for all aquaria, and this usually consists of ½ in (15mm) thick expanded polystyrene tiles or panels cut to the size of the tank base. This allows the tank, irrespective of its method of construction, to withstand all manner of jars, bendings and invisible adjustments which take place due to temperature changes and structural movements of the room.

Before accepting any tank from a dealer, give it a thorough inspection to check whether there are any scratches on the glass, as these are the starting points for bursts.

The above advice relates primarily to the decorative aquarium, but the design features apply equally to tanks for quarantine, temporary quarters, for breeding, and for the fish house. In the latter case it is useful to decide on a standard size in the interests of uniform appearance and the ease of obtaining quick replacements in emergencies.

Equipment

The few items of equipment required to maintain most coldwater aquaria are uncomplicated and inexpensive. Foremost is the net (you should have two or three), made of the softest possible nylon. Some consist of hard and sharp material which is abrasive to the scales of a fish and therefore a potential source of entry for skin infections. Green material seems more effective than white, as the fish seem to be less aware of it.

In coldwater aquaria algae do not usually build up very rapidly, but there is always an eventual accumulation of this disfigurement on the tank glass, so some form of scraper is essential. I prefer one with a razor blade which can be replaced when it gets blunt, but some users opt for versions which never scratch the glass or damage silicone seals, though the latter are by no means as effective. Algae magnets, far more expensive, are quite satisfactory in the early stages of algal formations, but are less effective against determined infestations.

After scraping algae away it is necessary to remove it from the tank floor (though some fish will obligingly eat it). This, together with surplus food scraps and accumulations of miscellaneous debris, may be disposed of either by means of a dip tube, for small, localized areas, or with the use of a siphon formed by a length of ½in (15mm) rubber tubing terminated by a fish tail attachment, for more general tidying.

One or two plastic buckets clearly marked 'FISH ONLY' will be needed to convey replacement water to the tanks and to receive the output from the siphon tubes when maintenance is being carried out.

All this activity involves dripping or splashing of water over carpets or furniture, but perfectly adequate protection can be obtained by the use of a few pieces of durable plastic sheeting, and pieces about 10ft (3m) long by 5ft (1½m) wide will prove very useful. A bag full of absorbent rag will enable you to mop up any spillage and to polish the front of tanks after servicing, as they usually get spattered with unsightly water droplets.

A jug or so should also be reserved for transferring replenishment water to the tank, though many aquarists prefer to siphon it direct from the bucket. Care must be taken that the buckets and jugs are not used for any other purposes whatever, as they could, accidentally, come into contact with insecticides and similar poisons, so they should always be kept in a safe place.

Water

Considering its prime place in fishkeeping generally, the many and varied eccentricities of water are not much of a worry to the cold-water fishkeeper. Tropical and marine enthusiasts are constantly concerned with water chemistry, because acidity and alkalinity levels and salt concentrations have drastic effects on the well-being of many of their charges. By contrast the coldwater aquarist may confidently go to his tap and use the mixture more or less as provided by the local water authority. Fluoridation is not detrimental in any way, and the only precaution which may need to be taken is to deal with chlorination if it seems to be excessive, and this is a simple matter. Since chlorine is an unstable gas it can be shaken out of solution very readily. This may be done by violently agitating the water by filling your buckets under the full force of the tap, or by using an appliance like a domestic food mixer to churn it. Small concentrations are harmless, and if you cannot smell the chlorine it is unlikely that the fish will suffer. Alternatively, the water may be left in the open for a day or so to naturalize.

When you have filled your new tank the water will appear to be buoyant, probably slightly cloudy, and there will be numbers of air bubbles on the side of the tank and on the furnishings. After it has been in use for a number of months it will begin to assume a heavier nature, reminiscent of white gin, rather oilier than in the early days. The main reason for this change is the loss of its former 'open' structure which included gases now dissipated, and the accumulation of natural exudations from the fish and other living contents of the tank, increasing the mineral content. The periodic removal of about a quarter of the water and its replacement by fresh water at the same temperature will do much to maintain healthy conditions and appearance.

If you can arrange to keep a water butt fed by uncontaminated rainwater you will find that, over a period, it will acquire numbers of living things like gnat larvae, bloodworms, *daphnia* and so on. This water will usually pass through various shades of green, according to the nature of the season, and the addition of some of it to your tanks will usually excite your fish. Placing an ailing fish in green water is often recommended by eminent aquarists, for reasons which cannot be fully understood, but there is little doubt that there is some tonic in this process. If you decide to use green water in your indoor tank for this purpose, you need not be concerned that the colour will remain as an unsightly feature, as it clears within a day or so. The addition of rain-water after a thunder-storm is also recommended due to its extreme buoyancy in these conditions.

Having established that normally available sources of water will pose no initial difficulties, we will now consider what processes may be necessary to keep it looking attractive and to serve the needs of the fish.

Aeration and filtration

Whatever the nature and size of your coldwater aquarium, it is an unnatural state of affairs, and its occupants are continually under stress of some sort. Any relief, therefore, is likely to result in improved health and performance of both fish and plants. So far as the fish are concerned, a primary requirement is the constant availability of enough oxygen for their routine functional purposes. They extract this from the water whilst it passes across capillaries in the gills during the course of respiration. Pollution, resulting in oxygen deficiency, can bring about loss of condition, gill damage, disease and death, depending on the degree to which it has advanced. Most of the oxygen extracted by the fish is replaced direct from the atmosphere, but this is not a very quick process, and anything which can speed it up or supplement it is a great help.

It is commonly believed that oxygenating plants contribute significantly to the addition of oxygen to the water, and that they also help to prevent imbalance by removing much of the carbon dioxide arising from the fish. This is not so, as if all plants are removed it will be found that this has little or no effect on the equilibrium of the tank. On the other hand, violent agitation of the

25

water surface, which serves to increase the surface area, will go a long way to maintaining a healthy tick-over. To achieve this, a reliable, fairly powerful and virtually noiseless air pump will be found to be a good investment, and it should be used at all times. If the noise becomes irritating the pump can sometimes be moved to a less used room or an outhouse. A length of airline tubing is used to connect the pump with the tank, and an airstone is fitted at the tank end. At some convenient point in the line a screw valve is inserted, so that the rate of flow can be adjusted. If several tanks are served from the same pump, a gang valve can be fitted, which is an arrangement to regulate the quantity of air supplied to each of them.

Oily-looking films often form on the water surface, and these seriously inhibit the ability of the water to absorb oxygen from the atmosphere. They are easily removed by drawing a sheet of newspaper across the water, applying successive sheets until all traces have disappeared.

Filtration of water may be carried out to achieve two ends. Firstly, some coldwater fish, notably the carps, are messy feeders and they fossick around on the tank floor for scraps of food, dislodging mud-like mulm, as it is termed, which clouds the water. This is unsightly but harmless in small quantities, and usually settles when the disturbance ceases. Secondly, fish excretions, especially of urine, cause the build-up of toxic mixtures which are invisible to us, and this insidious process can be nullified in large measure by properly regulated filtration. The usual ways of dealing with these conditions are by means of either internal or external filters, which are filled with layers of filter medium and activated charcoal. These need replenishing from time to time, depending on the throughput of water and the concentration of the detritus. The value of a good air pump is underlined if filters are used, as they are usually driven from this source. Alternatively, there are power filters driven by integral motors, which give a huge turnover of water at a high degree of efficiency. Their cost is very high by comparison with that of an unpowered filter unit, but on the other hand it is not necessary to run them all the time. Many aquarists use them to clear the water when it looks cloudy, and this is a rapid process. Care must always be taken not to discharge into the tank any water which has been standing for some time in the body of the power filter, as it is often highly polluted. It should be collected by ejecting the output into a bucket for a minute or so and then redirecting the output tube into the aquarium. Some fresh water should then be added to the tank to make good the quantity rejected.

Undergravel filtration is another method of conditioning, in which a perforated plastic plate on ¾in (20mm) supports is placed in the tank, to cover the complete floor area. One or more airlift tubes are attached to this plate, and they each contain an airline terminated by an airstone tuned to deliver fairly coarse bubbles. These give a heavy surge as they rise to the top of the airlift tube, thus causing water from the base of the tank to be set in motion so as to draw higher water downwards, and to circulate it. Two things are going on simultaneously with this type of filter. In the first place the oxygen/carbon dioxide exchange at the water surface is being speeded up, and in the second place colonies of bacteria which exist in the gravel covering the filter plate are maintained in a healthy state by the passage of water across them — the quicker

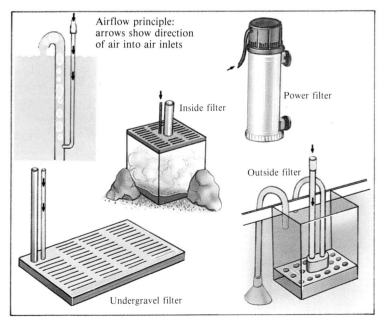

Airflow principle: arrows show direction of air into air inlets

Inside filter

Power filter

Outside filter

Undergravel filter

4 Filters

the flow, the better they thrive. This enables them to perform their function in life, which is the breaking down of the accumulated excretions of the fish into harmless combinations. This biological type of filter is efficient and cheap, but as it removes much of the mulm from the tank base it sometimes inhibits the growth of plants whose roots derive nourishment from it. In coldwater aquaria, where plant growth is often something of a difficulty, the power filter or the cheaper types of internal or external box filter will therefore prove most suitable.

Lighting

The lighting arrangements for decorative aquaria are usually housed on the underside of the tank hood, with the switches situated either at the rear of the hood or on a panel remote from it. In the latter case it is often convenient to incorporate them with the side panelling of a purpose-built cabinet. There are three types of lamp which are suitable for tank illumination — the tungsten striplight, the tungsten bulb, and the fluorescent tube. The aim should be to install over your show tanks a system of lighting which will not only give enough brightness for the plants to thrive, but also enable you to use units of it selectively, so as to achieve a variety of effects within the tank. This can range from a single lamp giving a highly dramatic effect, to a massed performance simulating high noon on a summer's day.

Tungsten lighting has a yellowish cast but it mixes effectively with fluorescent lamps which, themselves, give a variety of colour renderings. The best-known is marketed as the Gro Lux tube, which has a red bias and accentuates this colour in everything which it illuminates. It is said to be particularly suitable for plant growth, but those who buy it specially for this purpose often feel disappointed as it does not always achieve this end. This may be due to bad cultivation or unnoticed attacks on the plants by hungry fish. If you have to choose between tungsten and fluorescent lighting, the latter is the better option, because although the cost of equipment and tubes is high, the current consumption is quite low and the tubes have a long life. As tungsten bulbs emit a lot of heat they can give rise to undesirable temperature variations in the surface water in the tank unless a cover glass is interposed. Even so, they can cause this to crack under certain conditions. Bulbs also concentrate their light in 'hot spots', which results in a localization of algae and uneven plant growth, tailing away unattractively in the less favoured areas of the tank. For planning purposes a 40-watt lamp should be allowed for every 12in (30cm) of tank length if tungsten lighting is used. About 10-watts per 12in (30cm) will suffice if fluorescent lighting is chosen. The use of a cover glass between the water and the light source is recommended in order to prevent condensation from eroding the fittings, which are quite expensive to replace in the case of fluorescent lighting.

From the aesthetic point of view colour rendering fluorescent light really puts the coldwater tank on the map, and it does much to enhance the beauty of all types of goldfish, especially those with red in their pigmentation. There have been many converts to the hobby who have seen some of our native coldwater fish under this type of lighting for the first time. Roach and rudd are particularly notable for the glowing hues which can be achieved by this means.

The manipulation of a mixture of light sources to create maximum visual impact can be coupled with judicious positioning of surface plants within the tank. Highly lit areas can be contrasted with dimly visible caverns, and can be rearranged from time to time to suit the viewer. The fish too seem to prefer a series of spots with varying illumination. This particularly applies to any specimens introduced from the wild, which may take a little time to settle down, and which will appreciate shady retreats to which to retire if apparent danger threatens. Despite all precautions algal outbreaks can and do occur, and the fact that these can be controlled by reducing light means that the aquarist with a series of light sources above his tank can cope with this sort of nuisance quite easily, just by manipulating his switches. A dimmer control switch should also be considered with the same end in view.

Setting up the tank

Assuming that you have bought the largest tank you can afford, the setting up phase now begins with the mustering of the equipment already mentioned, together with plants and internal furnishing. An additional piece of equipment which will prove useful to the intending breeder is a combined heater/thermostat, as used in tropical aquaria, as this will be needed to speed up the hatching of eggs and the development of fry. This will be used in an unfurnished tank, so may be put in reserve until needed. Time spent on the aesthetics of coldwater decorative tanks is of very real importance, because they have to compete visually with their marine and warm water counterparts which, with their ready-made brilliance, are difficult to match. Nevertheless, the less garish but more intriguing effects which can be achieved by the thoughtful coldwater aquarist can more than compensate for nature's extravagance, and there are many who find subtle tones to be more restful and satisfying. Whilst there are no set scenarios for those who prefer fancy goldfish, the intending keeper of native species would do well to study their habits and to try to emulate a typical underwater setting. If local fish are to occupy the tank, pond or river material, including plant life, is easily obtained, looks authentic and is readily replenished. Nearly all aquatic plants will grow well without anything more than gravel in which to spread their roots: the addition of soil or peat, as well as being unnecessary, is likely to contribute to a muddy-looking water with which even the filters will be unable to cope. Coarse natural gravel, available from all aquarium shops, is most suitable for native species, but the various coloured artificial composts are extremely attractive, and may be used with devastating effect with fancy goldfish. Care must be taken not to put several different colours in one tank: the result is certainly a visual feast initially, but they get mixed up inseparably after a period of use and the resulting muddle is valueless as decoration.

Before setting the tank up in earnest it is advisable to put a number of pieces of cork bark into water to soak, so that they become waterlogged. This highly decorative substance yields very pleasing tones under water, especially with Gro Lux fluorescent lighting, and it is often associated with pieces of willow root, whose white, pink and red colouration blends well. Pieces of rockwork — these must all be of inert substances like granite, slate and coal — are then moved into approximate positions and shifted around until good 'fits' are achieved. Bogwood may also be used to supplement the underwater setting, and caverns, together with pockets in which plants may be set, should be constructed. A quantity of large pebbles or stones may be used to break up the foreground. The planning at this stage may be done dry, particularly if it is your first tank. Once you get a really pleasing arrangement, leave it overnight and look at it critically the following day, inviting comments from other members of the family. When a suitable panorama has been created, ensure that the higher pockets will in fact hold the gravel firmly when the water is added, as this is the real test of successful setting up. The beginner will find that it needs a lot of practice, and some aquarists advocate the use of pieces of wet clay to seal the bottom of these pockets. This treatment should be confined to the remoter spots in the tank where the fish will not root them out.

Although the gravel should be given a thorough wash under the tap before it is placed in the tank, this need not be too protracted as filtration quickly removes cloudiness. After it has been added it should be formed by hand into interesting contours, with the overall slope running from the rear of the tank towards the front. A saucer or plate should then be placed centrally on the gravel, and the water poured directly on to this, to avoid disturbing the foundations. This may be taken straight from the coldwater tap into one of the 'FISH ONLY' buckets, and thence transferred to the tank with a jug, or a clean hose may be used. The filling should be carried out in several stages, each leaving the water level at a point where it is possible to proceed with setting up work without unduly disturbing that which you have already done.

The plants should be inserted last of all. You should be very generous with them, observing that cheap plants are probably not worth having. Roots should be looking white and springy, and any which show signs of rotting must be discarded. The roots or bases of selected plants should be well tucked into the gravel in their intended positions, and groupings of similar plants should be built up gradually. Some aquarists use notched planting sticks to deploy their plants, but finger and thumb give you a much better feel for what is going on, and there is less danger of breaking brittle roots or stems this way. The value of lead weights or planting strips is debatable, and some find that rotting takes place where the collar is formed. Better results may be obtained by bending roots under heavy stones or rocks and pressing the gravel well down afterwards. The tank should be filled with water so that the surface becomes invisible when viewed from the front, and the level should be kept at that point.

If a filter and aerator are to be used they should be correctly positioned but not switched on. The cover glass should be laid in place, and the tank hood with the necessary lighting tubes fitted, should be placed on the very top, thus completing the main processes. The glass walls of the tank may sweat for a time, until the temperatures of the tank water and that of the room are the same, and you will notice lots of bubbles on the contents of the tank: these will gradually disperse. At this point extreme patience is required, because the plants need every extra day you can give them to put their roots down. A fortnight's settling period is not by any means too long, yet many people will put the fish in on the same day! It is worth noting that as the growth of plants is quicker than that of fish, there will be plenty of interest for the observer even in a fishless tank: the lack of disturbance will enable him to detect and remove any predators or pests like snails and he will be astonished at the increasing beauty of the plants themselves as they put on new foliage in step with the growing clarity of the water. The aerator and filter should be brought into operation a day or so before the fish take up residence.

5 Rockwork gives depth

Plants for the indoor coldwater aquarium

It is probably true to say that more fishkeepers have trouble in succeeding with plants than with fish, and the coldwater enthusiast starts with the added handicap that a high proportion of his favourite species — the carps — are herbivores, and they regard his lovingly displayed specimen plants as food rather than decoration. This difficulty can be overcome by ensuring that the plants have a reasonable chance of asserting themselves and, as explained earlier, a long settling-in period should be allowed. Even so, plants will not thrive if they have to compete with algae, nor will they withstand the attacks of the hundreds of snails which will eventually appear if so much as a single batch of eggs should penetrate the initial screening routine.

When buying plants for the coldwater tank you must make sure that they have been raised in cold water. Those collected from the wild or other known sources will be satisfactory from the acclimatization point of view, but they will be suspect as carriers of algae, snails and the eggs of predators. They should be immersed for several hours in a pan of tap water in which potassium permanganate crystals have been added so as to colour the solution deep pink, and then transferred to ordinary tap water for about a week. Examine them with a magnifying glass to see whether there are any signs of livestock, and pick off or rub away any visible algae. If there are still signs of snails or other pests like hydra, repeat the initial treatment or add a proprietary sterilizing agent at the recommended strength. Do not be misled by the fact that plants look clean as the germs of algae, together with a host of minute animal pests, are invisible to the naked eye.

Despite every care it may sometimes happen that the plants do not thrive, and this may be due to either excess or insufficient light. There is no sure formula here, and you will have to experiment with the light sources to arrive at an optimum coverage. As a guide, a single 20-watt fluorescent tube in a 24in (60cm) tank should be left on for about ten hours a day, but if algae begin to form, reduce the exposure by about a third. Conversely, if the plants show yellowing this may be due to insufficient light. Variations in plant well-being are also due to fluctuations in natural light and temperature. Unexpected results can arise from the effects of central heating and from draughts, so watch for these factors. A welfare measure taken by some experienced aquarists at the setting up stage is the insertion of peat 'plates' and loam beneath the gravel: the plates are pre-soaked until they become waterlogged, and they are then introduced into the tank so as to form pockets. These are filled with loam and the plants are carefully anchored in it. This is then covered by further suitably shaped plates, followed by the gravel.

The coldwater fishkeeper thus has plenty of scope for experimenting with plant culture, and the higher temperatures now prevailing in many homes because of central heating give him an opportunity to try out some of the more tolerant tropical species like Cryptocorynes which, if they succeed, can prove to be very decorative, as well as resistant to attack by the fish. Alternatively, some of the smaller pond marginals, even grass, may be tried in suitably strategic parts of the tank in order to achieve variety and changes of emphasis.

Submerged plants

Most of the following selected species of underwater plants are oxygenators to greater or lesser degree. Their main purpose is decoration, and in many cases they provide some form of food for herbivorous fish as well as accommodation for eggs and fry.
Sagittaria: There are several forms of this, including a giant variety which grows to about 20in (50cm). The leaves are long and narrow, between a ½ and ¾in (10 and 20mm) wide, and they rise to the surface from a common base, which should be planted just clear of the gravel. It reproduces by runners, and its glowing emerald green colouration makes it a distinguished plant for the rear of a tank or for a key feature in the middle regions.
Vallisneria: This is similar to *Sagittaria,* from which it is mainly distinguished by less emphatic veining in the leaves. It is a slighter plant too, with an extremely decorative variety *(V.torta),* the leaves of which twist their way in corkscrew fashion from the base. There are also red coloured varieties. This species is suitable for backgrounds, but as some fanciers have found difficulty in growing this in the same tank as *Sagittaria,* it may have to be used selectively.
Lagarosiphon: This used to be called *Elodea crispa.* It grows in long snake-like twists, often several feet long, and has series of

34

downward curling leaves, each about ¾in (20mm) long, arranged closely together and radiating from the central stem. It is rich green in colour and is a first-class oxygenator. As a prime target of carp, it loses many of its leaves as they browse on it, and its thick stem is thus left bare, but as it roots readily in mid water and usually grows quite rapidly, their depredations can usually be made good by cuttings which are simply plunged deeply into the gravel. It is a wonderful plant in the spawning tank, as the leaves seem to catch the eggs, and they give good shelter for fry.

Elodea: This is a similar plant to *Lagarosiphon,* but the leaves are straight instead of curved. There are two common forms, namely *E.densa,* with leaves about 1in (2.5cm) long on good specimens, and *E.canadensis,* whose leaves are only about two-thirds of that size. The former is a more choice species and is more restrained than *E.canadensis,* which often emulates *Lagarosiphon* in its spreading power.

Ceratophyllum: Commonly known as Hornwort, and appearing in both green and reddish forms, this is another very strong grower. The leaves are fine, hard, and rather brittle, radiating in whorls from the central stem. In the wild, terminal buds form late in the year and fall to the pond floor, whence they put forth new foliage in the spring. This is not a very good oxygenator but, like the next species, provides excellent cover for spawning.

Myriophyllum: Water Milfoil, this is a more handsome plant than Hornwort, which it closely resembles, but in this case the finely drawn leaves are more horizontal than in Hornwort, where they curve upwards. As an oxygenator it matches the *Elodeas,* and is extremely attractive in the aquarium because of its more delicate appearance and greater translucency. There are numerous forms, including some with red overtones. As in the case of the other fine leaved species mentioned, this plant will fail if there is much suspended debris in the water and if an excess of light causes an increase of algae, as both will settle on the leaves and result in complete collapse. Efficient filtration is therefore essential for its satisfactory culture in the average coldwater aquarium.

Ludwigia: A marsh plant rather than a submerged aquatic, this has thickish stems and pointed oval leaves which are often curled back on themselves and slightly fluted. Colourings cover a wide range, from light green to red, and often both colours occur in the same form, making it a fine subject for mass planting in a decorative tank. Under some conditions the lower leaves fall off, so allowance should be made for this by planting it where it will be partly screened by a feature such as a low rock. It may respond better to planting with peat plates and loam, and a long period should be allowed for rooting.

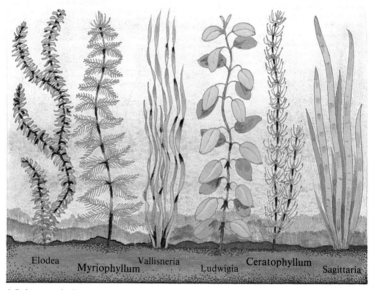

6 Submerged plants

Elodea Myriophyllum Vallisneria Ludwigia Ceratophyllum Sagittaria

Potamogeton: This is commonly known as Pondweed, and has leaves about 2in (5cm) long, arranged at intervals along a stem which can grow to several feet in length. They are rather long and narrow, often with wavy edges, and coloured deep green, brown or red. It resembles some forms of seaweed in general appearance, and is decorative rather than useful, as it is neither a very good oxygenator nor much of a spawning aid.

Fontinalis: The Willow Moss is a dark-hued, most attractive plant with thin stems and tiny leaves occurring throughout their length, which can reach 20in (50cm). Its value is high as a decorative plant in the tank foreground, where it should be set in clumps. As with the other fragile species, generous filtration is necessary to prevent saturation with loose debris, which soon flattens it. It is a first-class spawning receptacle and forms a secure hiding place into which many newly introduced fish will quickly penetrate, and in which they will remain until they have found their confidence.

Eleocharis: A choice and highly decorative species, Hairgrass is much sought after by aquarists seeking honours with decorative aquaria. It is light green in colour and grows naturally in shallow water, though the tank owner will use it completely submerged. Planted in small clumps, of which there should be several in the foreground of each tank, it is particularly effective, but it is not a very good doer and needs replenishing from time to time. If planted outside in the shallows of a pond, thickets may soon grow up, and supplies from such plantations may be used for the indoor aquarium, after proper cleansing measures have been taken.

Acorus: The dwarf versions of the Flags are splendid accent plants for all aquaria, and because their long pointed leaves are tough and their base rhizomes are sturdy, they stand up to a lot of rough treatment from the fish. They usually take a long time to increase in size, but at least they hold their own if given a proper settling-in period. There is an outstanding decorative form with variegated foliage, but this is not quite as tough as *A. calamus pusillus,* the commonly available green species.

Orontium aquaticum: The Golden Club of the garden pond, this is another choice and rather unusual plant for the larger aquarium, but it is worth trying as a feature. Long oval velvety green-blue floating leaves are later supplemented by longer, curved, ones from which a yellow tipped 'club' emerges.

Floating plants

There are several species of floating plant which can be used both as a decoration and as a regulator of overhead light reaching the submerged plantings. In the latter case, if the light is excessive, let the floating plants spread, otherwise thin every so often. The recommended species are *Lemna trisulca,* the Ivy Leaved Duckweed, and *Hydrocharis morsus-ranae,* the Frogbit. Both are pleasing and non-rampant species, and the carp, especially, will browse on the duckweed. Common Duckweed may be added from time to time as a further form of live fish food, but care must be taken to remove pests and predators from the undersides.

External plants

If tanks are housed on stands within the house, the general appearance will be made more attractive by the addition of shelving attached to the stand, on which containers of house plants may be stood. These will help to camouflage the usually unlovely lines of the average stand, and to take away the bleak edges of the tanks. Some of the hardiest and most uncomplaining of species include the Asparagus ferns, the *Chlorophytum*, which is variegated, and the *Tradescantias* which both trail and hang down from their pots, and which range in colour from light green to dark red. These will all thrive with neglect and are inexpensive. The more ambitious will make a feature of the 'garden round the tank', and include dwarf subjects like mosses, ferns and the like, together with more striking subjects like *Sansevieria* (Mother-in-Law's Tongue), whose bold pointed leaves fully complement the more subdued and diminutive species.

7 External (house) plants

Routine maintenance of aquaria

After the new aquarium has been allowed to mature and the fish have been introduced there begins one of the more difficult processes in keeping fish. It consists of getting into the habit of carrying out maintenance routines at the right time, all the time. If you manage to do this your aquaria will always look a picture and you will avoid the disillusionment which cumulative neglect will bring. The work involved is minimal, and the best way to ensure that you actually do it is to write in a diary or on a year planner the following operations, and to tick them off after you have completed them.

Weekly: Try to feed your fish with live food at least once a week, and to present different dried foods on the other days. The front glass of most tanks becomes dusty and spotted with dried droplets of water, and a thorough rub over with a damp chamois leather will restore its brilliance and clarity. The water level should be watched, and if it is visible when viewed from the front of the tank, fresh water, at the appropriate temperature, should be added. If feeding has been well regulated, there should be no surplus food on the floor of the tank, but remove any such, together with detritus, with a dip tube. In most tanks there will be some form of algal increase, and the tank scraper should be used to remove it from the inner surfaces of all the glass. Bearing in mind that all internal furnishings will eventually turn green if algae are not checked, dislodge all accumulations on rockwork and plants.

Monthly: A more thorough clean of the tank bottom should now be undertaken, using either a syphon tube with a fishtail attachment or a tank 'vacuum cleaner'. The latter is operated by joining it temporarily to an airline, and is a useful accessory which can be obtained from your dealer quite cheaply. A critical look should also be directed at the general appearance of the tank, and untidy plants should be trimmed: some unsightly gaps may have appeared, and these should be filled either by new purchases or by cuttings.

Quarterly: Airstones often get blocked after continuous use, and these should be examined for loss of efficiency. Replace any which cannot be improved after boiling them in water for ten minutes, or after scraping the surface gently with a file. If you maintain whiteworm cultures (*see* p.86), make a point of freshening them up by just stirring the earth with an old kitchen fork, and by topping up with new medium. Any cultures which are deteriorating badly should be tipped out, the worms removed and transferred to new compost. Keep a critical watch on the plants, aiming to improve on the concentration and diversity of plantings at each inspection.

Six monthly: Check over airlines and light fittings, and make sure that you have spares available in the event of failure. Any electrical connections which might have become chafed should be examined and repaired if necessary. If external plants are used for decoration they should be trimmed and the soil in the pots stirred gently, to ensure proper aeration. These should be replaced if growth is unsatisfactory, as struggling specimens detract from the aquarium instead of enhancing it.

Annually: Attention should be given to the general appearance and state of decoration of the aquarium stand or cabinet. Repolishing or painting may need to be carried out. If so, the work should be done in such a way that dangerous fumes are not allowed to collect in quantities which would affect the fish.

Leaks: These often occur if the water level falls, and will disappear if the tank is topped up promptly. Some leaks will 'weep' for days, and may respond to the application of cotton wool to which Araldite or clear nail varnish has been added. Cracks in the glass panels can sometimes be given emergency treatment by quickly wiping over the surface with an absorbent tissue and immediately applying Araldite, clear nail varnish or beeswax which has first been softened by warming. Whilst leaks in the putty can usually be cured (with patience), as described above, any damage to glass panels must be regarded seriously, especially in the case of large tanks. In certain conditions the glass may break unassisted along these lines, and complete replacement of the panel is recommended.

The Pond

The importance of proper planning has already been stressed — it is extremely difficult to undo the awful consequences of a hastily. built pond which has been wrongly placed. The site should be well away from trees, where root disturbance will upset foundations, and where leaf falls will lead to water pollution. If your garden is on a slope, the pond is better low than high because it is easier to push water downhill than up, and if your mains pressure is poor you could have filling or topping up problems. Front gardens in some areas are temptations for vandals and thieves, and purely for reasons of security secluded positions may be more satisfactory. You must decide whether the pond should be formal (usually round, oblong or square) or informal. The first of these options is best associated with a geometrically planned and conscientiously maintained garden, so for most of us the informal pond is the likely answer. Autumn is the best time to begin the project if results are wanted in the following season, as the hard work can be done during the off peak period of the gardening year. Think carefully about the sort of fish you wish to keep, as their needs will affect your method of construction. A mixed collection of goldfish and the more sedate species like carp and tench will require few trimmings, but a maximum water depth of 2ft (60cm) should be allowed. If you add orfe and similar oxygen loving fish like rudd and minnows you need a recirculating pump and possibly a water-fall. If you choose koi you should allow a depth of at least 3ft (90cm), preferably more. They will also, because of their mud-stirring habits, require a water filter, either in the form of a brick and concrete annexe, or a mechanical appliance as is used for swimming pools.

Types of pond

Puddled pools: If you have clay soil you will find it possible to practise the ancient monks' art of digging a hole, working the clay until it is like plasticine, and making a lining with it, nearly 1ft (30cm) thick. It is not very efficient but it is cheap and great fun, and if you do manage to make a good job of it the result equals some artificial methods.

Concrete ponds: Once the standard method, concrete ponds are now giving way to the challenge of the plastics industry, largely because they take longer to build, but also because badly made ones crack so easily and are difficult to repair without removing the contents. On the other hand, the precise shape you may be aiming for is more easily achieved with trowel and cement than with scissors and plastic sheeting, and this is the only type of pond in which internal features like overflows, outlets, filters and shelves for marginal plants can be integrated and properly built. When excavating, allowance should be made for up to 1ft (30cm) thickness of reinforced concrete, including final renderings, and the earth base must first be well consolidated by ramming. A 6in (15cm) layer of hardcore should then be added and well thumped into the earth. The whole pond should be held together by reinforcing bars and large meshed chicken wire, the former for the sides and the latter for the base and sides. Wooden or hardboard shuttering, oiled so that it will not stick to the concrete, should be used as moulds into which the wet concrete is poured. The mixture for this is three parts aggregate, two of sand and one of cement, by volume, and the pond base is usually made first, about 6in (15cm) to 8in (20cm) thick. It should be well tamped down to avoid air pockets, kept damp and allowed to dry slowly. Then the pond sides are dealt with, taking care that the chicken wire is kept as near to the middle of the concrete layer as possible. Tamp down each helping of concrete, as this will help to keep the wire rigid when successive quantities are added. It is essential to build a shelf for marginals within the greater part of the circumference of the pond; this must have a lip on its edge to contain any planting medium or pots, and to prevent them from falling to the pond floor.

An outer excavation may also be made for a bog garden, for which the total depth need not be much more than 1ft (30cm).

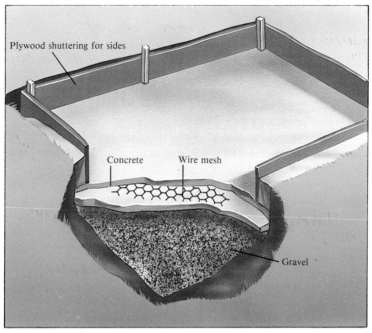

Plywood shuttering for sides

Concrete   Wire mesh

Gravel

8 Construction of concrete pond

Similar methods of construction may be employed as in the case of the pond, but at about half the thickness and with a minimum of reinforcing. Ideally, a bog garden should contain some water all the time, but the consequences of leaks are far less serious and repairs are more easily effected.

When the concrete has hardened the shuttering is removed and the walls are given a rendering, using a trowel, with a mixture of three parts sand to one of cement by volume, every effort being made to achieve a smooth finish. Sometimes a sloppy mixture of equal parts of sand and cement is then applied with a distemper brush, and well worked in. The final treatment is an application of either a commercial pond sealant (expensive) or egg preserver — waterglass — (very cheap), and in the latter case several coats should be applied. If no sealer has been used, several scrubbings and changes of fresh water must be made, in order to remove the free lime from the water which is fatal to fish. This is a dreadful waste of water, and is not entirely reliable as it is difficult to judge when it is completely safe. A carefully planned and executed concrete pond is a visual joy and is a most satisfying project to undertake: few other methods allow the craftsman to so obviously show his skill. When considering the cost, consult your neighbours. You may be able to hire and share concrete mixers or to order pre-mixed concrete in bulk. In the latter event a watchful eye on the weather chart may avoid despair on the day.

Preformed ponds: Fibre-glass or similar materials moulded into various formal or informal shapes simply require the excavation of a suitably sized hole, the removal of sharp stones and tree roots, and a lining of about 1in (2.5cm) of soft material, like sand, peat or wet newspaper. The pond shape is then inserted and filled with water. These mouldings are made in various colours and in modules which can be interlinked to form complexes of main ponds, watercourses and waterfalls. They are seldom sufficiently deep for the worst of our winters, and some form of protection may have to be applied unless the fish are removed for wintering indoors.

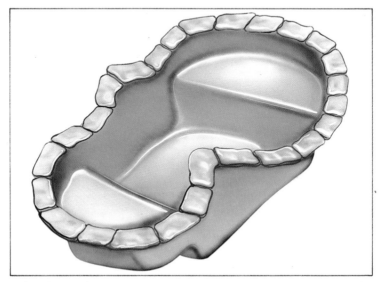

9 Fibreglass pond

Plastic sheeting: This ranges from heavy duty polythene, which is fairly cheap, to butyl rubber, which is quite expensive. The sheeting is simply laid into an excavation, created as described above for the preformed pond, and a heavy border of paving stones is laid down around the trimmed edge, to keep it in place and to provide a finished look. You pay here for longevity, as the cheap polythene lining will only last for a season or so because the material weathers badly at the waterline, becomes brittle and splits. Other types of sheeting incorporate a fabric base treated with a plastic, and these can last for twenty years or so. Butyl rubber, which is more flexible, has a life probably twice as long. All these sheetings can be fashioned into either formal or informal ponds by the most unskilled hands, and the results are usually quite pleasing. It is not possible to integrate overflows or to build in drainage taps as in the case of concrete ponds, but less permanent means can be contrived. The need for a lip on the shelf for marginal plants can be largely met by placing a row of clean bricks throughout its length. When deciding whether or not to use sheeting you should weigh up its extreme simplicity in construction against its comparative lack of adaptability. Once you have got the shape you have to live with it, and there are few variations which can be made. It is rather dangerous to walk around in these ponds during cleaning operations, in case you puncture the material. Repairs are possible, but if damage is below the waterline, such repairs cannot be expected to hold for ever. The formula for estimating the size of sheeting required is:

$$\frac{\text{Maximum length of excavation}}{+\ 2 \times \text{depth of pond}} = \text{length of liner}$$

$$\frac{\text{Maximum width of excavation}}{+\ 2 \times \text{depth of pond}} = \text{width of liner}$$

So a pond measuring 5 yards × 4 yards × 1 yard deep requires a liner measuring 7 yards × 6 yards.

Raised ponds: Although not automatically linked with any one of the above categories, these are normally only practicable if the ponds are made with concrete or sheeting. In this type of construction, compatible with either formal or informal styles, a wall is built to the chosen height all round the pond and topped with small paving stones. Pockets for rock plants may be incorporated by leaving gaps in the desired places. Such ponds offer greater safety where small children are likely to play nearby, as they are less likely to fall in, and they suit older folk too, as the fish and plants are brought nearer to their field of view without the need to bend down. Visually, they are more of a feature than a pond at ground level, which is often obscured by growing vegetation.

Size: A pond should be as big as you can afford it to be. It works out cheaper in the long run, as alterations and extensions to existing ponds are tiresome and awkward to effect, and the results are often prone to failure due to inexpert joining techniques.

10 Pool with waterfall

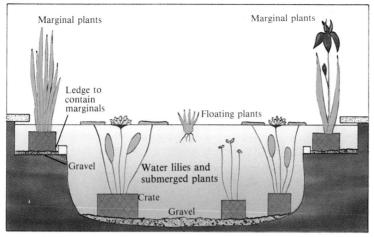

Marginal plants

Marginal plants

Ledge to
contain
marginals

Floating plants

Gravel

Water lilies and
submerged plants

Crate

Gravel

11 Planting the pool

Planting and filling the pond

It is sometimes recommended that loam or compost should be spread over the pond floor and in the shelf for marginals, and that this should be covered with gravel to prevent the fish from stirring it up and muddying the water. However, as fish grow they gradually acquire the strength to displace the gravel and delve around in the mud, so it is better to confine soil to the separate containers in which plants are usually accommodated; these take the form of plastic baskets obtainable in a range of sizes. Thus, it is more usual to line the pond floor and shelf with gravel to a depth of about 2in (5cm), and to place similar material on top of the soil used in the plant containers. The pond should be filled in stages, to allow easier positioning of plant containers. To prevent disturbance of gravel and planting medium, lay a sheet of polythene on the pond floor with a full bucket of water on top of it. The end of a garden hose should then be placed in the bucket and secured to the handle with a piece of wire, to direct the inflow to the bottom of the bucket. When the water has risen above the top of the bucket the latter may be removed and the water can be allowed to enter the pond direct. Make sure that the end of the hose is removed from the pond after filling, as it might otherwise act as a reverse syphon and empty it.

Pond maintenance routines

Ponds do not require the same degree of routine attention as do aquaria. In fact, as they usually look rather stark in outline for the first year or so, some healthy neglect will help them to weather and to blend with their surroundings. Nevertheless, there are certain annual landmarks.

In April there should be signs of activity amongst the fish, but do not begin feeding with prepared food until the fish rise to it. There is never harm in putting *daphnia* into the pond however as they will survive until the fish decide to feed. At this time in the spring the waterside plants should be trimmed, the soil should be weeded and overgrown clumps of plants may be divided and replanted. A complete clean out may be attempted if many fish were lost during the winter, as this would indicate fouling, and although autumn is the best time for this job, there could be further trouble during the summer if this task is long delayed.

During the summer you should aim to feed the fish several times a week with earthworm or whiteworm. Pond pellets or flaked food should be given sparingly. The breeder will have quite rigid routines during this period, and these are described later. The general fishkeeper will be on the lookout for young fish and if they are found, some of the recommended fine foods may be added to the shallows of the pond where many of the fry will be sheltering amongst the tangled rootage and miscellaneous debris. Before going on holiday, and in dry periods, top up the pond with water, and if you have cats or similar predators about, drape garden netting over as much of the surface as possible. Any blanket weed should be removed by entangling it with a garden cane, by twisting until whole lumps are removed and consigned to the compost heap. As summer comes to an end, the fish will begin to eat more in readiness for the lean months ahead, and feeding may be increased to meet this need. If there are trees in the vicinity, netting covers should be placed over the pond, well in advance of leaf fall, because rotting vegetation under winter's ice is certain death to your fish.

In September consider whether the pond needs a complete clean. This should be undertaken every year or so, and as it is a messy job, a full weekend should be allowed in which to carry it out. Prepare some containers as temporary homes for the fish, using water from the pond. Some damp sacking should be spread around, in which to wrap plants to keep them moist. Lengths of clean polythene sheeting should also be placed on the lawn to protect it if it is the nearest flat surface on which the plant and lily crates are to be placed after their removal from the pond. After lowering the water by means of a pump or syphon, the fish may be netted and should be examined for any signs of disease. The underwater plants are wrapped gently in wet sacking. The marginals and water lilies should be thinned and thoroughly washed under the hose, to remove the evil smelling black mud. The water level should then be lowered as far as the mud will permit, and this may be removed with a bucket or bailer and put either on the compost heap or straight onto the garden. All snails should be destroyed on sight, and their eggs, adhering to the undersides of lily leaves, should be rubbed out. The shell of the pond should then be scrubbed thoroughly and lightly hosed over, after which the water should be thrown away. Examine the pond for weak spots and leaks, and repair them. The water lilies and marginals may then be put back — try them in different spots from their old locations. After partly refilling the pond, allow it to settle for a few days and then replace the submerged plants after removing all dead material. Then top up and leave again for a day or so before freeing the fish. Their containers should be floated in the pond for about an hour before their release, in order to equalize temperatures.

If a pond heater is to be used during icy weather, make sure that it is in working order. This useful device ensures that a hole is maintained in the ice throughout a freeze, which enables toxic gases to escape. Ice should never be broken forcibly unless it is quite thin, since the shock waves are harmful to fish, and holes can usually be made by placing a kettle of hot water on the ice and letting it melt its way through. If the water level below the ice can then be lowered an inch (two and a half centimetres) or so it will probably not freeze again. Alternatively, place a wooden box over the ice hole and cover the box with some old sacking or carpet. Even if this does not stop the hole from freezing over, the resultant ice will be quite thin and is easily removed from time to time.

During the winter the flagged surround to the pond can become dangerous and slippery because of the growth of algae. This can be killed off by watering with a solution of a tablespoonful of Jeyes fluid to 1 gallon (4.5 litres) of water, but take care that none gets into the pond. If there is thick ice on the pond and there are still lots of dead stems and leaves from the marginals protruding from it, hoe them off flush with the surface, as they are then very brittle, and the debris can be be collected with a wire rake.

Equipment for the pond

Pondkeeping does not call for much equipment, and the essentials are inexpensive. They include nets with either long or short handles, buckets, netting (for protection against leaves and predators), a pond heater for the winter months and some large pieces of polythene sheet. Access to the normal range of garden tools is also necessary: the hoe, for example, will enable you to pull out rampaging underwater plants in midsummer and to trim dead growth above the ice in the winter. There are one or two expensive items which are well worth considering. A recirculating pump is a good investment for those intending to keep oxygen-greedy fish like orfe, and a waterfall can be associated with it at little extra cost. In the case of koi an external brick or concrete filter chamber should be constructed incorporating a water inlet, a gravel filter bed and an outlet pipe leading back to the pond. Potentially ugly, this should be sited where it can be effectively screened from view by an evergreen shrub. Care should be taken that all electrical cables, even though they are of low voltage, are protected by heavy grade plastic conduit or hosepipe, and that these are laid in such a way that they will neither trip people nor be severed by the lawnmower or the turf edger.

An alternative to the brick built type of filter is the internal pump and filter, such as is used for swimming pools. This is simply connected to the electrical supply after it has been placed in the water. The cleansed water is returned to the pond via a sprinkler bar, which can be concealed beneath an overhang of rock. Essential for koi, filters are universally valuable as they contribute materially to the general well-being, but it is important that they are regularly cleaned out. A fountain, on the other hand, is little more than decorative and has no place in the informal pond, where it looks out of place. Also, water lilies do not thrive in moving water so its positioning has to be chosen with some care. It is a pleasant adjunct to the formal pond as long as restraint is exercised when choosing its size. For those who wish to achieve startling effects there is a range of underwater lighting, but it is expensive and of doubtful value to the economy of the pond, especially if it is overdone. Limited flood-lighting in shrubbery surrounding the pond can look most attractive, however, and is unlikely to worry the fish in any way.

The pond and its plants
There is a tremendous range of possible species and varieties — prior reference to a specialist grower's catalogue will prove more satisfactory than impulse buying from garden centres and aquatic dealers. Many plant varieties are rampant and invasive and you are better off without them, so it is wiser to pay more for quality plants marketed by growers who are able to advise you about the best ones for your particular requirements. Choicer species cost more, but they are a lasting pleasure and seldom get out of hand. Plants associated with the garden pond may be considered under the following headings:

Submerged plants: Earlier we dealt with suitable submerged plants for the aquarium and of these *Lagarosiphon, Elodea, Ceratophyllum, Myriophyllum, Potamogeton* and *Fontinalis* are equally suitable for the outdoor pond. They are best bunched and tied to a heavy stone and dropped gently into the pond. Although they have an oxygenating function their main purpose is to provide shelter, food and spawning facilities for the fish, and it will be found that they all increase quickly with the exception of *Fontinalis,* which is best placed in the shallows, where its charms can be properly appreciated. Thin them drastically when they begin to spread, otherwise the pond can become choked.

Aponogeton distachyus, the Water Hawthorn, is a magnificent underwater plant from South Africa, which grows from tubers and throws strap-shaped leaves to the surface, each averaging about 5in (12.5cm) by 1in (2.5cm). The white inflorescences, which are spotted with black, are long, boat-like in shape, and have a delightful vanilla perfume.

Water lilies — The important consideration in selecting these glorious plants is to buy the right colour for the site and the right type for the depth of pond which you have constructed. There are giants and dwarfs and some have a pleasant perfume, so selection is very much a matter of personal choice. Do not be tempted to accept cuttings from friends unless the characteristics of the exporting and the importing ponds are comparable. They should be planted in plastic crates or baskets, or in plastic bowls in which holes have first been bored. Heavy loam and bonemeal is a good planting medium, and if you can invert an old piece of turf and place it on top of the container, this will help to give the plant a good start. Lily leaves should be in contact with the water surface until the plant has established itself, so rest the container on supports and gradually lower them from week to week until it ultimately reaches the bottom of the pond.

12 Waterlilies

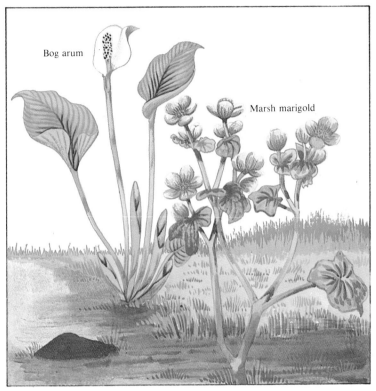

Bog arum

Marsh marigold

13 Marsh marigold and Bog arum

Marginal plants: These grow in a few inches of water on the shelf which projects inwards from the pond's perimeter. Alternatively, some can be planted in separate containers which are then lowered to the bottom of the pond. It is advisable to plant all marginals in a container of some sort because this restricts their spread and makes it easier for you with withdraw them from the water for maintenance, like trimming and splitting. About 4in (10cm) of compost (loam and bonemeal) is about right for most species, and after firmly planting each specimen, add about 1¼in (3.12cm) of gravel to the top of the container to prevent muddying once the fish have been introduced. Some of the better species will include *Calla palustris,* the Bog Arum, with shining heart-shaped leaves,

14 Irises, Arrowhead, Pickerel weed.

an attractive perfume, and a white flower resembling the florist's Arum Lily. *Caltha palustris,* the Marsh Marigold, has a splendid yellow-golden flower surmounting a low growing plant with shining rounded leaves. The double variety is especially worthwhile. *Iris laevigata* and *Iris kaempferi,* both Japanese Iris, provide a range of very refreshing colour, including yellow, blue and white, and the sword-shaped leaves stand proudly from the water for much of the season, rarely causing trouble by overgrowing their allotted space. *Juncus effusus spiralis* is an odd looking rush growing in a grotesque twisted fashion, reaching about 18in (45cm) in height, and it is always a talking point with visitors.

Mimulus or Musk is a low growing plant with trumpet-shaped flowers, usually yellow speckled with maroon, but there is a good range of attractive hybrids. This is not a very stable plant and it does need periodically replacing. *Orontium aquaticum*, the Golden Club, already described earlier, is one of the very finest of marginal plants, and although it can spread to cover a wide area it needs some coaxing to get it going. *Pontederia cordata*, or Pickerel Weed, has arrow-shaped leaves and the most beautiful powdery blue flowers. This grows to about 2ft (60cm) and looks particularly attractive when planted near the centre of the pond, but it needs a lot of sun and light to fully develop its flowers. *Sagittaria sagittifolia*, or Arrowhead, has white flowers and an arrow-shaped leaf, growing to a little over 1ft (30cm). *Scirpus zebrinus*, or the Zebra Rush, is an extremely fine plant which tops 3ft (90cm) when established. It has a long quilled leaf, alternately and horizontally barred with light green and white. As with all variegated plants, if completely green leaves appear, they should be removed. *Typha minima* is a dwarf Reedmace, wrongly called 'Bulrush'. It grows to a little over 1ft (30cm) and bears the well-loved reddish-brown elongated heads. *Typha angustifolia* is an alternative, reaching about 3ft (90cm). Other reed maces and bulrushes should be avoided because of their rampant nature.

Bog plants: The bog garden can simply consist of about 6in (15cm) of soil placed on top of an area of plastic sheeting in which a few holes have been punched. It is flooded at times and dry at others, but it is as well to try to keep it damp, even though this may mean the occasional use of the hose. In small gardens this area should be restrained because many of the most suitable species for such situations quickly choke all competitors, and you might find some of the bog species spreading into the shelf for the marginals. Unchecked, this could become a thorough nuisance. Some of the more respectable species include *Aconitum* or Monkshood, the blue delphinium-like flowers of which are long-lasting and resist rain. This grows to about 4ft (120cm). *Astilbes* and *Spiraeas* have high feathery flowers above finely cut foliage, and they grow to the same height as *Aconitum*, to which they are a good foil. *Hemerocallis*, or Day Lily, has long fleshy leaves and glorious orange flowers held on straight stems some 2ft (60cm) high. It needs reducing in girth about every second year. Many colour variations rather more peat, and varieties with coloured foliage will give remarkably attractive contrasts of shade and texture. Dwarf conifers ranging in shape from pyramids and tall spires to squat and sprawling subjects will break up the overall lines and, as they grow, will assume a quiet significance of their own. They rarely need more than a hosing to keep them fresh, and the lack of leaf fall makes them ideal for planting near water. The one deciduous tree which could be associated here is Young's Weeping Silver Birch, which should be allowed to dip its small and delicate leaves into the shallows. Its pleasing shape and contrasting bark are ample compensation for the trouble of netting against the autumn leaves.

Ponds for children

As conventional ponds can be dangerous where children are concerned, and vice versa, it is a good idea to let young people have small ponds of their own, and old sinks or halved beer barrels prove to be very suitable. Initially they will probably develop into mere containers of muddy water and very little else, but when grown ups are seen attending to their own fish and plants, the children soon catch on. The containers should be made watertight by filling in all cracks and holes with cement or mastic and painting the interiors with pond sealant. The bottom should be covered with pea gravel and a few of the more restrained underwater plants may then be added, together with a pot containing a dwarf marginal like *Typha minima*. An exquisite miniature water lily, *Nymphaea pygmaea helvola*, which is small enough to be planted in a flower-pot, will complete the picture. Children probably derive more interest from trying to see intangible things rather than those which are very obvious, and for this reason goldfish may not be the most suitable choice of fish. The common Three Spined Stickleback is a great favourite: it can be caught quite easily by most youngsters with access to the countryside, and it breeds quite readily. Other small fish like roach, rudd or minnows are equally suitable in very small sizes. Children who are successful with simple arrangements like these should be encouraged to manage an indoor aquarium or something equally ambitious after a season's practical experience. That is how true pondkeepers are made.

Coldwater Fish for Aquarium and Pond

This chapter describes the species of coldwater fish normally available to the aquarist in this country. Some species and certain varieties are more suitable in the aquarium than in the pond, and some are best kept on their own. Some are markedly more decorative, whilst others will breed more reliably than the rest. These characteristics will all be highlighted and they should be considered carefully before you decide what and how many to buy or to catch. As to the question of when to obtain fish, aquarium specimens may be acquired and introduced throughout the year, whilst pond fish are best handled between late spring, when the water should be beginning to warm up, and late summer, which will give them time to settle down before the onset of the colder weather.

Before making a final selection it may be useful to draw the distinction once again between the two main categories of fish — those which are slower-moving like goldfish and tench, and which are quite happy in still water, and those like orfe, roach and dace, which only really thrive in more highly oxygenated water, such as exists in well understocked environments or where there are water conditioning arrangements like mechanical circulating and filtering facilities. From the aesthetic point of view some fish-keepers prefer the mysteries of species with quieter colours, and like to peer into the water to watch them go about their affairs, whilst other fanciers require the stimulus of the more obviously attractive species which have been bred for their decorative value. The subdivision above gives some clue as to feeding habits: the former, largely vegetarian except before breeding, do not normally pursue flies at the surface, but the latter spend much of exist as hybrids. *Hostas* are impressive foliage plants, usually growing to about 2ft (60cm), with less significant flowers formed into spikes well above the leaves. They look most delicate, and indeed suffer considerably from slug damage in their early development. Well worth a little extra trouble, they gradually increase from year to year, and this is to be encouraged rather than curbed. *Lobelia cardinalis* is a plant with narrow leaves and a flower spike which rises to about 2ft (60cm). The individual flowers are of the most vivid red imaginable, and the species is best planted in a group for maximum effect. It is tender, so should be grown in a plastic pot, plunged into the bog garden during the summer, and lifted in entirety and put in the greenhouse to winter safely. *Primula denticulata,* with a high, ball-shaped flower head also does well in damp situations, and there are many other varieties of primula to choose from. Another group of plants admirably suited to the damper areas surrounding the pond are the ferns, of which the Hart's Tongue *(Scolopendrium vulgare)* and the Wall Spleenwort *(Asplenium trichomanes)* are particularly attractive.

Floating plants
Provided that it is not full of tiny snails, Duckweed is a welcome addition to the pond because the carp family love to eat it. *Azolla,* or Fairy Moss, in a range of colours from red to light green, is an attractive and fast spreading addition during the summer months, and a small quantity should be moved indoors to overwinter. *Riccia fluitans,* or Crystalwort, is a bright green mossy plant which grows rapidly under strong light and forms excellent hideaways for young fish. It should be treated as *Azolla* during the winter. The Frogbit, *Hydrocharis morsus-ranae,* is a charming plant with small round glossy leaves and a white flower, which never asserts itself and needs protection from snails if it is to become established.

Plant pests
Apart from Greenfly, there are remarkably few pests and diseases which seriously afflict aquatic plants. As these little creatures are excellent fish food they should be washed from the leaves with a brisk hosing into the pond, where they will be turned to very good purpose.

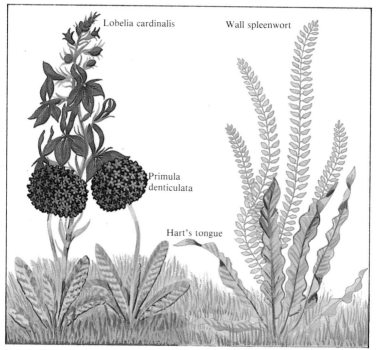

15 Lobelia cardinalis, Primula denticulata, Hart's tongue, Wall spleenwort.

Background to the pond

The soil taken from the excavation is usually well utilised by forming it into a hillock to back or partly encompass the pond. Whilst a wide selection of alpine plants can be grown on what usually becomes a rockery, many of them are not significant enough in shape to provide accents to the overall picture, and some pondkeepers turn to conventional garden plants to add greater interest. This can be a great mistake, as nasturtiums and roses clash with the colours of goldfish, and more subdued subjects will be found to blend better. A most effective background can be achieved by building a peat garden, using peat blocks to construct the main contours, and then filling the resultant boxes with a mixture of granulated peat and soil. Winter flowering heathers *(Ericas)* may be planted to form a glowing mat of colour during the dark months, when the fish are resting. These may be interplanted with some of the summer flowering heaths *(Callunas)* requiring their time at or near the surface stalking every small living thing, which they snap up with lightning speed and gracefulness. Koi, because of their gross feeding habits, fall into the second category, requiring specialized methods of management.

The Goldfish *(Carassius auratus)* is a member of the *Cyprinidae,* a huge family of carps and minnows of some two thousand species, typified by the lack of teeth in the jaws; they are in fact present in the throat. Since we are interested in several of the carps as suitable pond and aquarium species it is useful to differentiate between the genus *Carassius,* to which the Goldfish belongs, and the genus *Cyprinus,* which comprises the true Carps. The practical difference is that the former do not possess barbels, whilst the latter have four, attached to the upper lip. The fish with barbels tend to spend more of their time stirring and grubbing the base of the pond or tank, whilst those without them seem rather less prone to the habit. Here lies one of the main differences between goldfish and koi: the latter belongs to the genus *Cyprinus,* and its management requirements are significantly different from the quite modest needs of the Common Goldfish.

The Carps have an interesting history, ranging over the centuries, for there is ample evidence that man has cultivated certain species for food or for decoration, sometimes for both, from very early times. The Goldfish came to us from China and developed from what was originally a dark brown fish. As early as the fourth-century it was recorded that some of these fish showed red colouration, and this characteristic was developed by breeders into an acceptable decorative form. By about 1500 this had reached Japan and, as variations in shape were now also appearing, it was becoming very clear that here was a very malleable species indeed for the patient and the inventive to work upon. It reached Europe in the eighteenth century, and by the 1920's variations like the Shubunkin and the Oranda were being bred in this country. Such were the possibilities of variation in shape and colour that attempts were made over the years to codify them into show standards, and in this country the Goldfish Society of Great Britain published a booklet on the subject in 1950, which has had a number of revisions since then. This only deals with a number of forms which are acceptable in the United Kingdom, but there are well over a hundred others, mainly confined to the Far East, which we rarely even see. The basic varieties of fancy goldfish now recognized by the G.S.G.B. fall into the following eight categories:

Type	Characteristics
a G.S.G.B. Bristol type Shubunkin and Goldfish	Have a single tail
b Veiltail	Anal and tail fins are divided and flowing
c Globe Eye	The eyes protrude
d Pearlscale	Scales have a domed appearance
e Bramblehead	The head is covered with a bramble-like growth
f Celestial	Eyes protrude and look heavenwards
g Pompon	Nasal septa distended
h Bubble Eye	Bubble-like sacs below the eyes

The purpose of these is to define and encourage true breeding techniques, but cognizance has also been taken of five other popular varieties, and standards have been drawn up for the Oranda, Fantail, London Shubunkin and Common Goldfish, Broadtail Moor and Comet.

All the above can be further classified under one of the following three groupings. These relate to the body appearance of the fish, which is dependent on the reflective properties of the tissues underlying the scales. These groups are: Metallic — Maximum reflectiveness, in which a burnished appearance is presented. Nacreous — A midway stage, in which there is a mother-of-pearl appearance. This used to be termed 'calico' or 'scaleless'. Matt — Minimum reflectiveness, giving a velvety appearance.

Of the many forms bred today, some are such extreme variations from the common ancestor that to many aquarists they are mere freaks of nature which never should have been allowed to survive. To the fancier, they are absolute perfection! So it is all a matter of taste.

The forms which meet with most general approval are the Shubunkin, the Comet, the Fantail and the Veiltail. Those with more bizarre features, often combined with laboured efforts at swimming, include the Moor, the Celestial, the Lionhead, the Oranda and the Jikin. Hardiness tends to diminish with the degree of variation from the common ancestor, and the more extreme forms are really more suitable for aquarium culture where they can be protected from extremely low temperature.

Returning to the Common Goldfish, it is a stocky, amiable and hardy creature, growing sometimes to 18in (45cm) in length, and becoming quite tame if strict feeding habits are established. It is equally at home in the tank and the pond and will eat a wide range of foods, though it prefers vegetable matter. It breeds readily, and indeed poses something of a difficulty in a thriving pond as to the limitation of numbers and preservation of quality. The former depends somewhat on the agility and ingenuity of the pond owner, as young fish are not all that easy to catch, but it will usually be left for natural influences to take their toll. Unfortunately many of the surviving fry revert to type, which simply means that they remain brown coloured for all their lives, and as some specimens take a season or so to achieve their final colours, thinning the stock can be quite perplexing. There are often black patches on goldfish, but this is usually a temporary feature, when the pigmentation is changing, and it usually disappears in time: it is in no way associated with ill health. The Goldfish is one of the most decorative of coldwater fish, as apart from the familiar gold colour, there are variations from near-white to red, together with many permutations of several colours. It is also a most congenial fish and has no unpleasant anti-social tendencies apart from an appetite for its own eggs and fry. The most popular varieties will now be discussed.

The Comet: This originated in the U.S.A., and resembles the Common Goldfish but has a sleeker outline and its finnage is much more impressive. The dorsal fin is pointed and flows away from the body, and is more concave than in the case of the goldfish. The tail is very long and forked, being held fully extended. There is a single anal fin, which is longer and more pointed than those of its near relation. Similar colour variations apply, and treatment and characteristics are exactly as ascribed to the goldfish. It has a reputation for being rather livelier than the other fancy varieties, and this enhances its value as a specimen for the pond, in which it performs rather better than in aquaria. It is a less good breeder in a tank than some of the less agile of fancy goldfish, possibly because of the restricted space available, so would-be breeders should provide really long tanks and well aerated water if it is to spawn successfully.

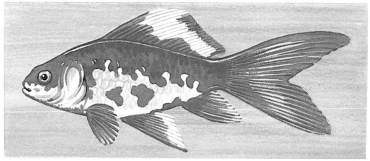

16 The Comet

The Shubunkin: This variation came into its own during the first quarter of the twentieth century, after having been developed by the Japanese. Its main characteristic is its nacreous appearance, which was formerly termed 'scaleless', 'calico' or 'mottled', and it consists of a light blue body shade superimposed by patches of other colours like red, orange and yellow, with a sprinkling of black. There are two forms: the London Shubunkin, with the same general shape as the Common Goldfish and with the same finnage; and the Bristol Shubunkin, with a similar body shape to the Comet, but with a broader tail and more rounded fins.

Both are treated as hardy and are extremely suitable for either tank or pond. The Bristol is the smaller of the two, and does not grow much above 6in (15cm), whereas the London can top 10in (25cm) under good conditions. Breeding is as easy as with the Common Goldfish, with which it will mate, but this should not be encouraged! It is a very showy fish, and the young tend to assume their colours (at least in part) during their first season. If these are brought indoors for the winter or are raised in an indoor tank, they make interesting exhibits during the darker months, rivalling the colourings of many of the tropicals, especially when viewed under Gro Lux lighting.

17 The Shubunkin and the Fantail

The Fantail: The body shape is oval and the dorsal fin is quite deep, nearing three quarters of the depth of the body. The tail fins consist of two large and erect fins joined at the top, and there is a double anal fin. Although it does not grow above about 4in (10cm) it is hardy enough to be left in deeper ponds over winter, and it certainly makes a very fine subject for the indoor tank, where it is easily bred. In order to maintain quality of stock, severe culling is necessary with this and the following more highly developed types of goldfish, in which the main faults are malformed finnage and body shapes. There are some accepted forms with protruding eyes.

The Veiltail: Here the body is spherical rather than oval. As with the Fantail, the dorsal is very deep. The tail and anal fins are divided, and all are longer than those of the Fantail. The tail is split into two long and flowing 'skirts', which are much longer than the body of the fish and are allowed to droop downwards in a way which does not occur in the varieties so far mentioned. This variety can grow to about 8in (20cm), including the tail, but the body size is always very small in proportion to the whole fish. It displays an appearance of extreme grace and delicacy and is indeed much less hardy than the forms already listed. It is best confined to the aquarium, though some enthusiasts turn them out into ponds during the warmer weather. Like all the long finned varieties care should be taken that aggressive fish are kept away from them, otherwise they will suffer fin damage. Even goldfish can be spiteful at times, so long tailed fish are best kept in tanks of their own. As with the Fantail, there are forms with protruding eyes.

18 The Moor

The Moor: A suitable companion for smaller specimens of Veiltail is the Moor, often termed the Telescopic Eyed Moor. It is a chubby black fish, always scaled, and with very prominent protruding eyes. It may assume the finnage of either the Fantail or the Veiltail. It rarely grows much above 5in (12.5cm) and is unsuited to pond life. As a form of contrast in a home aquarium containing some nicely coloured specimens of other long tailed varieties, it has no equal.

65

19 The Lionhead

The Lionhead: This and the following variety, typified by the bramble-like growth over the cap of the head, is for the specialist rather than the general fishkeeper, who is sometimes put off by the odd appearance of these and similar forms. The Lionhead has the body shape of the Veiltail, but it has no dorsal fin. Its other finnage is like that of the Fantail. Normally not growing larger than about 6in (15cm), it is very suitable for an indoor tank, and may be bred successfully where temperatures of 16−20C prevail. Owners of this and similar varieties speak highly of the endearing habits of individual fish, which become very tame in the aquarium.

The Oranda: Like the Lionhead this has a curiously wrinkled cap, but the nature of its body and finnage is otherwise similar to that of the Veiltail. It reacts to overall culture in the same way as the Lionhead, and breeds as readily.

Other fancy goldfish
Other varieties like the Celestial, in which the eyes are turned perpetually heavenwards, the Jikin, the Pom Pom and the Toad Head, to name but a few, demand management under sub-tropical conditions and they are usually kept and raised in quarters dedicated to each type. Breeding these highly developed forms results in many disappointments to the beginner because of the tiny proportion of fry which actually develop into acceptable fish. More experienced breeders become philosophical on this subject and count their blessings.

Other carp

The fish so far discussed have descended from *Carassius auratus,* which originated in the Orient. Further west, a near relative, the Crucian Carp, *Carassius carassius,* occurred in the wild form, mainly in Central Europe, but also in parts of the British Isles. It is similar in body shape to the Common Goldfish, but rather deeper, and has a greenish-brown back with paler underparts. There are bronze overtones on the back and on the fins. This is a quietly attractive fish, usually taken from the wild at a length of 4−6in (10−15cm), though it will grow much larger. It is amenable to both tank and pond conditions, and is quite easy to keep in good health as it eats almost anything. It is usually kept in ponds because it is supposedly too dull for aquarium conditions. This is quite a wrong assumption, as modern fluorescent lighting brings its several attractive tones into prominence, and it is worthy of a place in any mixed coldwater collection.

The Common Carp: *(Cyprinus carpio)* is the first member of the genus *Cyprinus* which we have so far considered for tank or pond. It is very similar in general form to the Crucian Carp but, in common with other members of this genus, it is distinguished by the presence of two barbels on each side of the upper lip. Its scales also seem rather more clearly defined. It originated in China and, like *Carassius,* was bred for both food and entertainment, mainly the former, as it can grow to an immense size, and lengths of 40in (100cm) have been recorded. In the course of selective breeding two interesting variations were produced, namely the Leather Carp and the Mirror Carp. Their names are apt descriptions, as the former has a matt and leathery exterior, and the latter possesses a number of large scales on the upper part of its body, which are metallic and reflect like mirrors. Small specimens of all three of these carp make interesting subjects for study, and are quite at home in the aquarium, where they will take food of every sort. They are less appreciated in a pond, but are quite harmless to other fish, and their air of lugubrious detachment nicely complements a mixed collection. The floor of tanks and ponds should not contain soil beneath the gravel, as these fish love to stir it up in their quest for food, and their presence is then detected by rising clouds of mud. Therefore, for members of this genus, a filtration system is sometimes used.

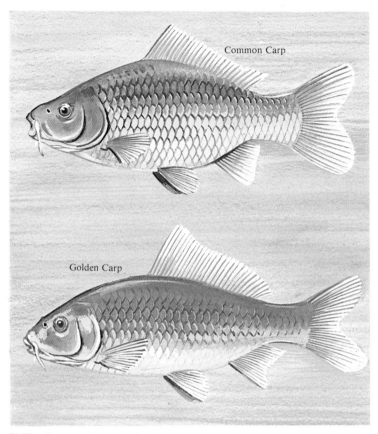

20 The Common Carp and the Golden Carp

The Golden Carp: Also known as Hi Goi, this is another variation of *Cyprinus carpio* which originated in China and was developed by the Japanese as an ornamental fish. It is reminiscent of a Common Goldfish with barbels, and makes an interesting alternative to it as a candidate for either tank or pond, provided that its mud stirring habits can be tolerated. They are available from specialist dealers, but seem to be in shorter supply than they deserve to be. Under good conditions they will grow to 20in (50cm), but under average pond conditions growth would tend to level out at about half that size.

21 A Koi

Koi: *(Nishiki-koi),* Rainbow or Brocaded Carp, are one of the results of centuries of selective breeding by the Japanese of members of the genus *Cyprinus,* and it is not known for certain when the types identifiable today first came into being. There does indeed seem to be some very mixed parentage between the genera *Carassius* and *Cyprinus* (further to complicate the issue), as some specimens have barbels and others have not. The fish are unquestionably the most attractive innovations to appear in the West this century, and many fishkeepers are now specializing in keeping them to the exclusion of all else. They can grow to about 24in (60cm) at a rate which exceeds that of most other carp, and nobody should contemplate keeping them unless a large pond can be provided. The fish are similar in shape to the Common Goldfish, but there is such a wide spectrum of scale and colour differentiation that here the resemblance ends. Some fish are self-coloured, some have two colours, and others have three. These are interplayed with four distinct types of scale formation — normal scales, a matt scaling, a brilliant metallic scaling, and irregular scaling reminiscent of the Mirror Carp. Some of the more usual colour combinations are *Kohaku* (red on white), *Sanke* (black and red mottle on white ground) and *Hi-utsuri* (red on black).

Koi require a pond at least 10ft (3m) long and about 4ft (1¼ m) deep, which allows for adequate swimway and safe overwintering. They are extremely heavy eaters and will remove all but the toughest plant life, only water lilies being able to withstand their constant attack. Water filtration and circulation must be incorporated in the pond design if clear water is to be maintained, but no actual harm will befall the fish if their owner is indifferent to the unpleasant appearance of the muddy water which will otherwise form a feature of the pond during the warmer months of the year. Because of their rapid growth rate koi are not really suitable for tank conditions, and even when kept in ponds their habits run counter to those of so many other fish that they should really be kept on their own. The larger and choicer specimens can cost hundreds of pounds, but breeding is not a short cut to quick fortunes because perhaps only one or two fish per spawning have quality. Most others are throwbacks and should be destroyed. Unfortunately much rubbish is offered throughout the trade and it gives the koi a bad name, so never buy koi unless you have expert guidance. Like the other carp, koi become very tame and make delightful pets, perhaps more obviously so in the case of the larger specimens. There is increasing evidence that imported koi require quarantine periods of several months, whereas home-produced stock is much more reliable. It is also noted that if koi are kept in heated ponds during the winter, their growth rate will be maintained. Outdoor heated ponds are quite uneconomic in this climate and most specimens will be perfectly safe during the coldest winters provided that the water is sufficiently deep and that it is free of pollution. Knowledge of this variety is being acquired all the time, and membership of the British Koi Keepers' Society is recommended to all intending purchasers. Keeping koi is something of an undertaking and a responsibility, and this Society will provide current and balanced information to enable enquirers to make up their own minds whether this highly enjoyable branch of the hobby is within their capability.

The Tench: *(Tinca tinca)* is a highly individual fish, occurring in a normal form which is dark olive green or black on the upper body, shading to yellowish tones on the underparts, and in a variation which is largely golden above and yellowish below. It has a rather slimy body with very tiny scales and adopts a slightly sickle-shaped stance when at rest in mid water. Equipped with barbels, it spends much of its time on the bottom, but creates far less muddy water than the carp. It is completely compatible with other fish, but as neither form swims in the upper water very often, these fish are seen to best advantage in aquaria, in which 4in (10cm) specimens will prove to be an ideal size. In the wild a length of 27in (67.5cm) can be reached. Omnivorous, this species is easy to keep and is an excellent contrast to goldfish varieties.

The foregoing fish are tolerant of the normal, still-water pond (with the exception of the koi, which have been described in this section because of their relationship with the other carp). The following species, often kept under these conditions nevertheless do better in systems with recirculating and aerating equipment, especially if breeding results are desired.

22 The Tench

The Orfe: *(Idus idus)* is unusual in that it occurs naturally in both golden and silver forms. It is a long and graceful fish with shoaling habits, but it seems to take a long time before it reaches spawning size. It is generally available for sale in sizes from about 2½in (6.25cm) upwards, and it is the golden form which is most preferred by aquarists. It often bears black blotches, which tend to disappear with age. Though the smaller specimens are suitable for tank life, they grow very quickly and will not thrive unless provided with plenty of room. Any fish which are outgrowing their surroundings should be given the run of a pond in the spring as soon as the water has begun to warm up. Orfe prefer live food, but will rise to pelleted food and similar fare as willingly as goldfish. They are exceptionally showy and fast moving and can reach 30in (75cm) in the wild. Spawning is likely when the fish are about 10in (25cm), which emphasizes the need to allow them generous accommodation.

23 The Rudd

The Rudd: *(Scardinius erythrophthalmus)* is a slightly stockier species than the Orfe, but is one of the most beautiful natives of our ponds and rivers, feeding on a variety of small animal life as well as aquatic plants. The upper parts are bluish-green, paling below, and the fins have red overtones. The eyes are yellow, which helps to differentiate this from the Roach, with which it is often confused, whose eyes are red. Another shoaling fish, this can reach 16in (40cm), but small specimens are highly suitable for either tank or pond. They breed when at about 6in (15cm), and are usually obtained from the wild, rarely being offered for sale. The Golden Rudd, a variant, is a slight misnomer, as it is more reddish than the name would suggest and often has darker patches on the upper body. This is usually obtainable from the trade.

The Roach: *(Rutilus rutilus)* is very similar to the Rudd, but has more olive colourings and the eyes are red. Its habits are much the same as those of the Rudd, but it finds less favour with the aquarist because of its quieter colouring. There is only one colour form.

The Dace: *(Leuciscus leuciscus)* grows to about 12in (30cm) in the wild, and is another of the lively shoaling fish of our rivers which is usually collected rather than bought. It is a leaden colour above and silvery below, and at about 4in (10cm) is a good companion fish to orfe and rudd, whose shoaling habits it emulates. Not very showy, this is nevertheless a desirable acquisition for both tank and pond where good clear water with plenty of movement can be maintained.

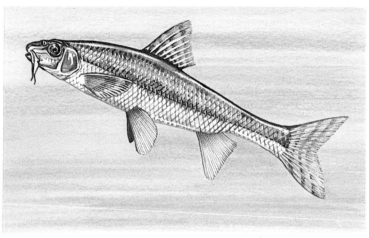

24 The Gudgeon

The Gudgeon: *(Gobio gobio)* is a species which rarely exceeds 6in (15cm), and therefore fits conveniently into both tank and pond. It is flattish, usually with brown overtones and black or brown markings, and it has barbels. It is a most charming denizen of the lower water, and its large eyes are very becoming. Omnivorous, it is probably best studied in the aquarium and given the freedom of the pond when it has overgrown its surroundings. It is harmless to other fish, excepting fry, and is easy to keep. Rarely available commercially, these fish are not difficult to catch from either still or running water. They will live happily in both the still pond and the conditioned one, but do rather better in the latter.

The Minnow: *(Phoxinus phoxinus)* is a familiar resident of running water and can grow to 6in (15cm), but is usually found at less than half this size. It has mainly buff and olive overtones, with black, brown and red markings in a wide selection of combinations. Its shoaling habits are very entertaining, and it is an inquisitive and wholly likeable species, best appreciated in a very highly aerated tank set aside for its exclusive use. Given a good selection of live food it is reasonably easy to breed under such conditions. In a pond it could be something of a nuisance to breeding fish, but the gorgeous nuptial colouring of the male make it worth giving it a small pond to itself, in which it will provide endless entertainment to the onlooker.

25 The Bitterling

The Bitterling: *(Rhodeus sericeus)* rarely grows above 4in (10cm), but it is one of the choicest of all the naturally occurring European species. It is normally grey-green above, with silver undersides, and it has a dark stripe from the base of the tail to the middle of the body. In the breeding season, the male gradually assumes a most extraordinary range of brilliant colour, including violet and red. Even in normal times these fish look gorgeous under Gro Lux lighting, and for these reasons alone they are best kept in a tank because their charms are somewhat dissipated in the average pond. The breeding habits described later in the book are fascinating. Management is quite easy as these fish are not fussy about food, and they can usually be obtained from specialist dealers in coldwater fish.

The following species are recommended for aquaria rather than ponds because they are aggressive in the presence of other fish, often particularly so to unwanted members of their own kind.

The Perch: *(Perca fluviatilis).* A bony fish, the Perch is a most attractive species with a rather deep body and double dorsal fins. It is grey-green above and yellowish below, with vertical black bands and rainbow colourings around the gill plates. It has a deliberate motion through the water, pausing after each progression as though to take stock of the situation. Nervy at first in captivity, it can become very tame, and as it is largely carnivorous its food supply must be carefully planned.

Sticklebacks: *(Gasterosteus aculeatus)* the Three Spined Stickle-back is obtainable from many waters throughout the country, and is familiar as a rather bony and gaunt little fish, the male of which develops a resplendent red throat during the breeding season. The nesting habits are particularly interesting to students, and they may be observed in springtime if a pair is given a large tank to themselves. A continuous supply of live food is necessary, and if conditions are suitable they will eventually grow to about 4in (10cm).

26 The Stickleback

The Bass family: Small specimens of the Peacock Eyed Bass, the Sunfish, the Black Bass and the Diamond Bass make excellent subjects for the coldwater aquarium. They originate from North America, where they reach large sizes. They are fussy about water conditions, which they require to be quite hard, and as they are carnivorous they are rather more difficult to manage than some of the foregoing species. However, they are content with unaerated water, and they become quite tame after settling down. The Peacock Eyed Bass is the most beautiful of this group and a number can be kept in the same tank. All the others are scrappy and are best treated on the basis of one species per tank. They are rather difficult to come by at present in this country, and deserve a return to vogue.

Fellow travellers and foes

Aquaria are not often visited by unwelcome creatures excepting snails, and these should be destroyed promptly unless plant growth is rampant enough to withstand their attacks. The pond, however, is under constant bombardment by insect life during the warmer weather, and numerous animals visit it the whole year round. Breeding ponds are usually made in squares or oblongs for ease of management, and it is a simple matter to construct frames of fine meshed material to exclude everything but small flies, which are valuable as food.

The garden pond therefore becomes the home of unwelcome creatures like the nymph of the dragonfly and of charming ones like newts. It provides a drink for scores of birds and for water-collecting honeybees. Pond skaters, beetles, water boatmen and Mayflies will all be found there, and in favoured situations the toad and the frog will come to spawn in the spring. Some will cause the loss of young fish, whilst others will simply provide added interest to the onlooker. It is best to settle on a policy of letting nature have its way, for most losses have their compensations. The lovely grass snake may be seen basking on the lily pads and the dragonfly will repay its ravagings with spellbinding aerobatics. The birds will bring their young to drink. These are very worth-while things, and they add the final touch to the living pond.

Even so, we sometimes have to take defensive measures. Cats are a terrible nuisance, and can be deterred only by dogs or water, so try to construct the pond surround in such a way that they do not get near enough to scoop the fish out. Herons may be kept away by stretching netting loosely above the water, supporting it if necessary by long bamboo canes, and the kingfisher will also respond to this, though treatment may in this case need to be prolonged because they are more firmly resident in a locality than the heron, which is somewhat opportunist. Nylon line should not be used to repel animals as it can get twisted round the legs of well intentioned birds and this may kill them.

Ill-informed dealers will sometimes advise the addition of the American Catfish and of mussels to your pond, both in the rôle of scavengers. This should be resisted firmly, as the former is a dreadful predator and the latter simply plough up the bottom and foul the water when they die.

Breeding Coldwater Fish

Whilst many tropical fish are quite easy to breed at any time of the year in the United Kingdom, because of the simulated exotic environment in which we keep them, coldwater species are much less prolific in captivity, and their cycle of reproduction waxes and wanes with the passage of the seasons. A reasonable measure of success may nevertheless occur in the average garden pond, where fish breed under virtually natural conditons. However, we must recognize the fundamental difference between 'artificial' fish like goldfish and koi, which do not breed true to type, and 'natural' species like rudd and tench, which do. The individual goldfish and koi which the fancier values must conform to the shapes and colours specified in show standards and specialist equivalents, and the proportion of each spawning which comes anywhere near to such criteria is extremely small. So we are fighting nature all the time in trying to produce acceptable artificial fish, and the specimens which fall short of the approved vital statistics are rejected. Nature, perversely, tends to kill off the types we have cultivated and encourages reversion to the original wild and relatively uninteresting fish from which the modern varieties have been derived by selective breeding. The breeder of goldfish and koi therefore has the task of controlling the reproduction of his stock, or sorting and classifying the offspring, and of disposing of throwbacks. The latter process, known as culling, may involve killing the worst rejects. The owner of the 'natural' species like tench or roach has none of these decisions to take. One day he will suddenly notice that there are young fish in the pond, as the spawnings are usually unobtrusive, and he will then spend quite a lot of time trying to identify the parents. Such uncontrolled breeding is a useful means of replenishing the natural losses of one's stock, but predators of one sort or another rule out this method as a reliable technique for raising large quantities of fish.

Controlled breeding, therefore, in which the parents and breeding quarters are preselected, is the most satisfactory way of generating new stock, and it is particularly successful as applied to the goldfish in its many forms. Whilst there are variations in practice by individual breeders, the annual cycle described here does achieve reasonably hardy strains. Hardiness is a relative quality though, and many aquarists regularly bring their more valuable stock into shelter during the winter.

Breeding of the Common Goldfish begins indoors — this usually implies the availability of a fish house or a fish room — in about March or April, when the water temperature can be maintained comfortably at about 16C. Adult stock should then be showing improved colours, the female fish appearing increasingly plump with the formation of spawn, and the males beginning to display white tubercles on the gill covers and sometimes elsewhere on the body. The sexes should be separated and fed copiously on live food for two or three weeks, longer if possible. A breeding tank of at least 13 gallons (60 litres) should be set up and half filled with water, as breeding fish prefer the shallows. Large bunches of plants like *Myriophyllum* or *Fontinalis,* or spawning mops 6in (15cm) lengths of nylon knitting wool tied together in the centre so as to form a ball), are then placed in the water and the female fish is introduced. In the evening of the following day the male is added to the tank, and some chasing will probably occur. Spawning should take place early the next morning, and both of the fish must be removed when it is evident that the female is spent, otherwise most of the eggs will be eaten. A thermostat/ heater should then be placed in the tank and the temperature gently raised to about 21C, at which the fry will hatch in three to four days. Higher temperatures should not be attempted because they result in poorer quality fish. The fry hang on to underwater surfaces for about two days, during which time they absorb the contents of the yolk sac, which looks like a greatly bulging stomach, and then begin tentative and erratic attempts to propel themselves through the water. This is a critical period and many sink to the floor of the tank and fail to make the grade. As soon as this stage is reached they should be fed with newly hatched brine shrimp and limited quantities of hard boiled egg yolk squeezed through a piece of fine cloth. Later, microworm may be offered. As the fry gain in size they will take Grindal worm, and when they are a month old they should receive their first sorting. This is mainly to give them more space to develop, but poor specimens should certainly be destroyed during this formative period.

The beginner will find a magnifying glass very useful in the quest for good and bad points, and the help of local fellow enthusiasts will usually be offered to the apprentice who is willing to learn his craft. As the season progresses more and more space should be given to the growing fish, and the temperature should be lowered to normal levels. The aim should be to give the fish an extra boost in feeding in the autumn, and to winter them under cover, maintaining temperatures just above freezing point. By the following spring they will have completed a cycle under near natural conditions and can then be subjected to normal management standards.

The beginner with an appetite whetted by the breeding of some common goldfish or shubunkins will note that some characteristics take a long time to develop, and final culling may take place in later seasons. The more exotic forms of fancy goldfish can only be obtained from specialist dealers and from some private breeders, who will give good advice to purchasers of these particular fish. In buying these comparative rarities it is not necessary to pay top prices because even lower grade specimens of a good strain will throw some quality offspring. Their survival will then depend on the skill applied in recognizing them during the processes of inspecting, culling and growing on.

Koi, increasingly in demand as a pond fish, has breeding habits similar to those of the goldfish, but because its breeding size is about 12in (30cm) it is usually spawned in a pond rather than a tank. It is a species requiring large and deep ponds and it should be kept to itself. Even goldfish are doubtful companions as they will interbreed, further complicating the task of producing specimens of passable quality, only about one per cent of each spawning normally consisting of worthwhile specimens. Outdoor ponds dedicated to adult pairs of many species of fish will give good results if they contain no furnishings other than spawning mops and plants like *Myriophyllum*. When spawnings have been observed the mops or plants bearing the eggs may be removed from the pond to indoor aquaria, where the eggs may be treated as in the case of goldfish. Small reserve ponds or containers should always be available for the reception of growing fry, whose need for space is as urgent as it is for food. Some breeders simply remove the breeding pair from the pond, leaving the eggs to hatch *in situ*. The results here are fewer raised fish, but they are probably hardier than those which receive artificial stimuli in their early days.

In the home aquarium there are several species which will provide spectacular breeding displays. The Bitterling, which will be quite happy in a 13 gallon (60 litre) tank, is not difficult to sex, and it has the unusual characteristic of depositing its eggs in a freshwater mussel — the Painter's Mussel *(Unio pictorum)* — via a long ovipositor extruded by the female during the breeding period. The young fish hatch within the mussel and are ejected, free swimming, about five weeks after the eggs are laid. They should be offered brine shrimp and microworm.

Sticklebacks, easily obtained from many ponds and lakes, are gorgeous in the breeding season, when the male assumes its conspicuous red throat. The territorial and paternal approach by this little fish to the round nest of debris and to the subsequent baby fish are characteristics of this underrated species of which many people are completely unaware.

The Sunfish and Bass which originate from North America are rarely bred in the home aquarium because the specimens of suitable size for the tank are not really adult. Smaller species like the Peacock Eyed Bass, the most beautiful of this group, might succeed in alkaline water in a tank with a sandy floor and a number of rocks and plant thickets. Depressions are excavated and the eggs are laid within them. The female should be removed and the brood left to the care of the male.

Breeding of coldwater fish is a tremendously interesting pastime, and is quite a challenge because of the difficulty in sexing the majority of species which have been described in this book. It is best to buy five or six fish and to grow them on, with breeding in mind. They should be conditioned with the best available live food and given plenty of room. Then, when they are of breeding size, they will sort themselves out.

Feeding

Dietitians have scorned the ant 'egg' as a fish food for some decades, pointing out its almost total lack of nutrients and its inherent unattractiveness to fish. Yet for many years this is nearly all that was available to the goldfish, and somehow it managed to survive. This fact is a high tribute to the hardiness of the species rather than to the food. There is now a wide selection of dried, freeze dried and frozen food, balanced according to the nature of the intended recipient, and suitably graded to fit the individual mouth. Let us consider the main constituents of foodstuffs. Protein is needed for body building, carbohydrate for energy, fat for wintering, minerals for such processes as bone maintenance, and vitamins for aiding the discharge of a number of normal bodily functions. Suitable variations in the proportions of these may be offered to differing groups of fish at differing stages of development with optimum benefit, and the packages you buy across the counter reflect these permutations. At the same time it is quite safe to experiment by feeding, say, marine food to goldfish and vice versa. Colourants are sometimes incorporated which excite the fish into exotic hues, but such cosmetics should be treated with caution as they are likely to mask the initial onset of ill health.

The process of feeding fish is a highly pleasurable matter, and the shrewd owner will always allow himself enough time to observe all that goes on. Likes and dislikes can be detected, and the diet adjusted accordingly. Food which is rejected is not only costly but potentially dangerous if it is left to decay on the bottom of the tank or pond. Fish are at their liveliest when they are subjected to a wide choice of food, even though some items may take time to achieve full appeal. If feeding times are adhered to punctually, most fish will virtually queue up for the next meal, and many will become finger tame. Carp, especially koi, can be handled at such times, even to the point of lifting them out of the water!

Whatever type of dried food you use, it must be fresh and unsullied. Dampness is most damaging, and all proprietary foods must be kept in airtight containers in a cool and dry situation, preferably in a locker where pests and poisonous sprays can be excluded. Although the 'Jumbo' packages of food will prove economical for the owner of large collections of fish, the average aquarist will find it better to buy several different brands in the smaller containers. On no account should food be offered to fish if it displays any signs of mould, or if it suddenly smells different from usual.

A watchful eye at feeding time will also reveal whether bullying fish are getting more than their fair share and whether the feeding technique may need adjusting in favour of the more reticent specimens. Many aquarists use a feeding ring anchored in one spot in the tank, and this can be helpful in assessing when more food needs to be added, and it certainly aids tank hygiene by localizing unwanted fragments which collect beneath it and can be removed easily with a syphon. On the other hand, aggressive fish find it easy to monopolize the restricted area provided by these rings, and it may be found preferable to remove the control altogether, and to allow the food to find its own level. This usually turns out to be the tank bottom, and in the case of the carp family it is an ideal place for titbits, which they obligingly remove during the course of their routine searchings of the gravel.

Fish eat more when the water is warm, which is of some importance to the pondkeeper. When the thermometer stands at 10C fish may begin to feed, but below this they should be left to their own devices. At around 19C they may be expected to consume above average quantities, but even though a pond is less easy to pollute than a tank, overfeeding should never occur. Early autumn is an important time for fish overwintering outside, as they seem to anticipate the stresses of the hard times ahead by feeding steadily, weather permitting, thereby building up a reserve. Absences during holidays can be catered for quite easily. It is often recommended that fish be left unfed for anything up to a fortnight, and though this is perfectly reasonable as applied to ponds, in which there is a continuous natural addition of flies and the like, I can see no justification for denying tank fish their food simply because one may fear that friends and neighbours acting in *loco parentis* may overfeed their charges and kill them. Clearly written instructions, supplemented by a sticky label affixed to each tank, giving the exact amount required, is all that is needed. A tin of the most popular staple food is then left in a convenient position, with a tiny spoon alongside (a salt spoon is ideal). The dosage per day or every other day is then prescribed as a proportion or multiple of this unit. It is unfair to expect non-fishkeepers to have to deal with the feeding of live food, so if you have young fish to rear or breeding pairs to condition during your absence, it is better to work out a mutual aid arrangement with a member of the local club.

Types of food
Three main classes may be said to exist, as follows: proprietary fish food, which may be dried, freeze dried or frozen; adaptations of domestic foodstuffs; live or natural food.

Proprietary fish food: This is usually marketed as a staple diet for the type of fish in question, and it is constructed in flake, granule or pellet form, the latter usually being intended for use in ponds. It is highly reliable as it takes severe overfeeding to pollute the average tank, and it is extremely attractive to the fish. The flake forms are readily adaptable to fish of all sizes, as the segments can be either left alone or rubbed down between finger and thumb; some granular food unfortunately tends to sink rather too quickly for species which prefer to feed at the surface. Whilst pond pellets are becoming increasingly popular they should be used with some discrimination. They contain a high protein element, and there is some evidence that their use results in obesity, which is a far less desirable feature than the accelerated growth rate which they set out to achieve. It seems likely, however, that they are quite safe is used sparingly. I do not recommend scattering quantities on the pond surface and letting the fish just pick at them. They take some time to break down, and you can never be quite sure how much has actually been consumed. A way of assessing this is to allow a number of pellets to soak for a while, and to flick them into the pond after gently squeezing the water out of them. They disintegrate on hitting the water and the fish rise to them immediately.

Freeze dried and frozen food is much more specialized, and

83

consists of processed natural subjects like *Daphnia, Tubifex* and Brine Shrimp. These are useful to break sequences of staple food, and are usually relished. Frozen food is treated to remove potential disease or predator organisms commonly associated with the live versions, but it has to be stored in a refrigerator or freezer, and this may not be convenient to everyone, even today. It should be thawed out before being offered to the fish, and as it sinks quite rapidly, a watch must be kept that no appreciable surplus builds up. Some hardened breeders still compound their own magic mixes which can either be frozen or baked into blocks and fed dry. For the most part such recipes are a doubtful economy, and I would recommend them only to specialists and to those with plenty of time on their hands.

Adapted domestic foodstuffs: These may take simple forms like scraped or chopped lean meat, liver and heart. White fish is also very good, and hard herring roe will often send fish frantic. Provided that fatty substances are avoided (fats and oils give rise to scums on the water surface and interrupt the oxygen/carbon dioxide interchange) there is a long list of other possibilities, including Bemax, mashed potato, porridge, hard boiled egg yolk, spinach, cauliflower, fish paste and vermicelli. The larger fish will accept many substances simply chopped to a size which they can ingest, but it will sometimes be possible to drop in larger material, like boiled lettuce leaves, which they can pick at. A liquidizer is invaluable in reducing many ingredients to purée form, which is particularly acceptable to young and growing fish and, of course, the contents of many baby food tins may be used to similar effect. Tinned pet meat has been shown to be a highly successful diet for some of the larger pond fish, but great care must be taken to exclude the fatty elements.

Live and natural food: The former is defined as cultivated or collected material, and the latter as food which already exists in the environment of the fish, and on which they will feed whether we wish them to or not. Here we are mainly considering animal contributions to diet, but it should be remembered that many plants and algae are also consumed, especially by the carps. A fish will nibble any plant it takes a fancy to, and we need take no special action apart from planting the tank or pond as recommended elsewhere in this book.

A few pieces of equipment will be needed for the collection, maintenance and preparation of most of these foods, and if the best use is to be made of them, a few unpleasant disciplines will have to be mastered — but it is worthwhile, for within this group of foods lies the key to much of the real success in fishkeeping, notably the breeding and rearing of specimens of distinction. A fine meshed net on a long handle will trap most of the species mentioned, and a bucket acts as a suitable container during collecting expeditions. A number of expanded polystyrene boxes (about 10in x 5in x 5in (25cm x 12.5cm x 12.5cm)) will house the worm cultures, and some small paste pots will be useful for microworms. A few wooden boxes about 5in (12.5cm) deep and 10in (25cm) square will also serve as culture containers, and some medicine droppers are aids to the introduction of foods like infusoria and brine shrimp to the fish tanks. The most sinister apparatus is a cutting board and a razor sharp handicraft knife, which are used to reduce worms of various sorts to manageable size. There are also worm shredders on the market, which make the reduction process somewhat more tolerable to the squeamish, but some folk just cannot face the surgery involved and prefer to confine their attentions to the inert foods mentioned above or to such live foods as can be served much as they come. The main groups are listed below, very roughly in descending order of size.

Earthworms: The optimum size is about 2½in (6.25cm), and they seem to be in finest condition when taken from moist, recently manured, soil. They are probably the best of all live foods, proving excellent for bringing breeding fish into full condition. Chopping or shredding is essential in most cases, but large pond fish will take them whole. Winter supplies can be maintained by filling a wooden box with fibrous compost and adding a plentiful supply of small worms, towards the end of the summer. The box should be placed in a frostproof place with a number of tree leaves scattered over the surface. A damp sack over these and a piece of glass on top completes the process. During dry periods, patches of earth about 3ft (90cm) square should be copiously watered, and tea leaves strewn on the surface, which should then be covered with a damp sack. A sheet of wood on top of this will help to conserve the vital moisture. Worms may be coaxed from underground by watering the soil with a thin mixture of mustard and water or with a weak solution of permanganate of potash in water; the worms will soon come to the surface and should be washed before feeding them to the fish.

Tubifex worms: These thread-like creatures are usually about 2½−3in (6.25−7.5cm) long and spend most of their existence undulating their pinkish-red bodies to and fro above the river and pond mud in which they are anchored. They are at their best near sewage outfalls, so many aquarists are wary of using them for fear of introducing harmful organisms, and they seldom occur elsewhere in sufficient quantity to justify collection, which is a messy and time consuming undertaking. Most aquatic dealers sell them but their availability fluctuates with extremes of weather, so they are not a reliable form of live food for much of the year. They should be thoroughly cleaned by placing them into a bowl and exposing them to the full force of the jet of the cold water tap. This will fragment the ball formation which they naturally assume after capture, and any detritus, being lighter, can be floated off. Several washes are needed. They are then allowed to reunite as a ball, and this can be placed in a shallow container (like a soup plate) with very little water in it, which is stood in a cool place, preferably under a dripping tap, to keep fresh. Quantities of worms may be pulled away with tweezers and either fed direct to the fish or cut into appropriate sizes.

Flies: These are inevitable contributions to diet in the pond, but the tank or fish house owner may wish to use them as a variant indoors for larger fish. The larvae can usually be bought from angling shops as 'gentles', and hatched out in jam jars with perforated lids. The larvae may, of course, be fed to the fish, and it would be interesting to note whether any of the dyes used to colour them increases their appeal to captive fish. Greenfly may be collected from the garden for the benefit of the smaller fish, provided that it has not come into contact with any garden insecticide.

Caterpillars and other garden insects: Smooth caterpillars will usually be accepted by pond fish, but avoid the hairy ones. Beetles, slaters and woodlice may also be tried on the larger fish.

Whiteworm: (Enchytrae), or whiteworm, are naturally found in decaying leaf mould, and measure about ¾in (18mm). They are thin, milky-white and slow moving. Their great attribute is the speed with which they reproduce their kind, which makes them a cheap and reliable food source for nearly all fish. Perhaps the best way to start is with a commercially provided culture, which may be broken into several parts and used to infect compost in your own containers. Wooden boxes, earthenware bowls and expanded polystyrene boxes are quite suitable, and should be about 8in (20cm) square and 5in (12.5cm) deep. A damp mixture of fibrous loam and peat is then inserted within about 1in (2.5cm) of the top, and the infection should be mixed quite thoroughly into this. A small piece of stale bread, moistened with milk or water, is then placed in a small hollow in the middle of the surface of the mixture to act as food for the worms. A piece of glass about 5in (12.5cm) square should then be laid on top of the soil, and the culture is completed by placing a piece of hardboard or lino on the very top, cut so as to allow about ¾in (18mm) between it and the edge of the container. This mix should then be left for several weeks to allow the worms to reproduce, and when they are seen clinging to the underside of the piece of glass they may be removed in gradually increasing quantities. The bread should be replaced as soon as it has been consumed, great care being taken that any fragments displaying mildew are removed without delay. Whiteworm are usually chopped before being given to fish, and some observers have noted that they tend to pass through digestive systems complete if treated otherwise. As fish have a keen sense of smell, it is highly likely that chopped segments are more exciting than whole worms. After a while the cultures may become muddy and yield less well, so steps should be taken all the time to prepare reserve boxes by infecting them from stock, which they will, in due course, completely replace. The length of the life of cultures varies considerably, but they are best kept under shade, where the temperatures are low in summer, and where the moisture level is maintained. Whiteworm is nearly always eagerly taken by healthy fish, and it may be fed regularly, but since it has a fattening effect, it should not be overdone.

Water Shrimp (Gammarus) and *Water Louse (Asellus):* These crustaceans, which reach about ¾in (18mm), are commonly found in ditches and streams, and if they can be captured in sufficient quantity, constitute a welcome diet change for larger fish. Introduced into the pond, they might even form their own colonies and produce limited quantities of small offspring, useful in a raising pond, but less welcome where there are spawnings. *Phantom (Chaoborus), Gnat (Culex)* and *Midge (Chironomus)* larvae: These are valuable foods for medium to large fish, but can seldom be collected in sufficient quantity to make much impact. The Phantom (or Glassworm) may be collected for most of the year, even in winter, and appears as a transparent glassy cylinder in mid-water, from which it can be extracted quite easily with a net. Gnat larvae appear in still water during the summer months, and are seen hanging downwards from the water surface, disappearing swiftly with loop-like jerks to the depths just as you are about to catch them. The trick is to sweep the net through the water as they are on their return trip to the surface. Bloodworms are the larval form of the midge, and these are less easy to collect in quantity, as they spend some time in tube-like shelters of mud. A water butt is an ideal source of gnat and midge larvae, and the warmer the weather, the more steadily they multiply. They reach a length of about ½ – ¾ in (12 – 18mm).

Grindal Worm: This is very similar to whiteworm in general appearance, but reaching only half its size. It should be kept under warmer conditions, about 20C suiting it best. The culture boxes can be smaller too and fine oatmeal and similar farinaceous products may be used, cooked or uncooked, as food for the worms. Grindal is suitable for smaller fish or for fry in advanced stages and, as with *enchytrae,* it may prove to be more effective if it is chopped before being given to the fish.

Wingless Fruit Flies: These are another welcome variation for small and medium-sized fish, but they are a little more trouble to raise than worms. Several large-sized jars are needed, with close fitting fabric tops. Rotting fruit or special mixes containing yeast are placed in the jars and a number of flies are added to each. In time, according to the temperature at which the cultures are maintained, surpluses will appear, which can be decanted directly into the tank water.

Daphnia and *Cyclops:* These minute crustaceans which grow to about 1/10in (2mm) are the delight of the breeder, because they seem to give so much pleasure as well as condition to his stock and their offspring alike. *Cyclops* are usually a pale fawn colour and are less common than *daphnia,* which appear in huge clouds in waters such as cattle ponds, where there is a presence of suspended algae. In such green water conditions they multiply amazingly quickly, and may be collected quite simply by means of a few deft sweeps with a fine meshed net. Catches should be examined carefully for the presence of pests like *hydra* and predatory larvae, but if these are absent it is quite safe to feed *daphnia* to your fish after a quick swirl of the net through fresh clean water. These creatures assume a variety of colours, the most usual being buff, but red, green and almost black specimens are quite often met with. They move through the water in a continuous series of jerks, whilst *cyclops* tend to remain still for longer periods before proceeding in more purposeful spurts. If you allow green water to develop in a large container in your garden, the addition of a few *daphnia* will yield good dividends, but as soon as the water clears the swarm should be removed and a fresh culture of green water started. Keep this water covered with fine material like muslin to exclude predatory larvae, which soon decimate the contents. Newts too will clear a culture very rapidly. The smaller sizes of *cyclops* and *daphnia,* screened through fine meshed netting, are invaluable for growing fry.

Micro Worms: We are now nearing the end of the size scale and succeeding foods are used mainly in the rearing of fry. Micro worms are minute creatures about 1/20in (1½mm) long, and they reproduce themselves in their thousands in very restricted spaces. Obtain a culture from a fellow aquarist or from a dealer (though few of the latter have them readily available). About six small paste pots are needed, and these are used in rotation because cultures only last for a week or so: the aim is to have a third at full strength, a third working to their prime, and the remainder just beginning to reproduce. The food for the worms is cooked porridge, and a spoonful is placed in the container. To the top of this is added an infection of microworm, just visible to the naked eye as a moving mass. These worms are then allowed to proliferate for a day or so, but in the meantime a number of pieces of matchstick or iced lolly stick, of a suitable size to place within the pot, should be soaked in water until waterlogged. This is because microworm are attracted to damp wood, and if a few of the soaked pieces are stacked on top of the porridge, the worms will gradually insinuate themselves upwards to the highest layer, which may then be picked off and swirled through the tank water, releasing thousands of them for the fish to eat. A more controlled method of feeding is to wash off the worms into a cupful of tank water, and to transfer this via a medicine dropper to the tank housing the fry, at regular intervals. This is an exceptionally valuable source of food for young fish, and may be fed continuously until it proves to be too small to attract attention. Like the other worms, it remains alive under water for some time, and is therefore not a potential source of pollution: indeed it acts as a good reserve against the missed feeding which even the most diligent aquarist has to accept at times. A similar food, micro eels, is smaller than microworm, and has the advantage that it may be poured direct from the culture jar into the tank of fry.

Brine Shrimp (Artemia salina):   The shrimp in the Great Lakes of the U.S.A. are so prolific that their eggs can be collected in huge quantities, and dried and packaged with a minimum of processing. They are easily hatched under artificial conditions, and the emergent young, termed nauplii, are of prime value as starter food for many species of fish. The reddish-brown eggs are poured into water containing a tablespoonful of sea salt to about 7 pints (4 litres) of water, and they hatch within about forty-eight hours at 20C. The resultant red cloud of rapidly dancing minute shrimp is gathered with stocking-fine netting, quickly washed in fresh water, and then added to the tank of fry. When it is desired to feed small quantities, perhaps because there are few fry to satisfy, they may be held for a few hours in a separate container in a brackish solution. The method of hatching these eggs should be so arranged that the nauplii are kept separate from the empty shells and from unhatched eggs, as these can be harmful to young fish if they are ingested. Since the nauplii are attracted by light, a separation can be achieved by using a sandwich-box with a darkened compart-ment in which the eggs are initially placed, and from which the live young shrimp will swim as soon as light is made available in the adjoining section. Aeration increases the percentage hatch. There are several commercially available hatching devices, and these are inexpensive. The San Francisco type of brine shrimp is smaller than the others, and has proved to be outstandingly successful when feeding the tiniest fry. In some cases there are failures of fry because of the ill effects of protracted saline intake, so a watch must be kept for any increasing mortality rate, in which event a switch must be made to microworm or finely chopped Grindal worm, which can be continued indefinitely without harmful effects.

Infusoria: This is the general term given to the microscopic organisms which occur naturally in water, and whose life cycles can be speeded up to the advantage of the aquarist, given suitable culture conditions. Usually several jars of pond water are stood outside and decaying lettuce leaves are added to them. The decomposition of these substances aids the reproduction of the infusoria, which appear as slowly moving clouds after a few days. A succession of containers is needed to maintain continuity. The organisms are fed to the tank containing the fry via a slow syphon, the flow rate being adjusted in such a way that a steady output is disposed of by the young fish, avoiding any build-up which might cause pollution and consequential losses. There are also liquid fry foods on the market, which are added direct to the water. As these are highly concentrated, only a few drops are needed for each feed, and these are swirled around vigorously in the water to distribute their constituents. The fry ingest some of these and the remainder encourage a build-up of the infusoria already in the water, which the fry likewise dispose of. However, infusoria feeding can be a risky business because of the delicate balance required within the breeding tank, and in many cases today brine shrimp has become the starter food, par excellence.

Some Useful Data

DATA FOR AQUARIUM size 24in × 12in × 12in (60cm × 30cm × 30cm) — litres 54, gallons 12; weight kg 55; stocked weight kg 75; surface area sq cm 1800; gravel kg 12.

HEATER/THERMOSTAT for above — for breeding purposes, or for maintaining ideal cold water temperature of 15C (60F) — 100w rating.

A 2 gallon bucket holds about 12kg (26lb) of sand or gravel.

LIGHTING REQUIREMENTS —
Tungsten — watts = 32 × length in inches of tank
Number of hours illuminated
or 40w per 12in (30cm) of tank length for ten hours per day.
Fluorescent — ¼ of wattage resulting from above formulae.

WATTAGE OF FLUORESCENT TUBES — 21in (52.5cm) = 13w; 24in (60cm) = 20w.

CONCRETE — Amount required for pond with 6in (15cm) thick shell:
divide 60 into total square footage of bottom and all sides to obtain number of cubic yards of concrete needed. Mix should be, by volume, 1 of cement, 2 of sand, and 3 of aggregate.
A cubic yard of concrete requires about 5¼cwt cement, 9¾cwt sand and 19½cwt aggregate.

POND CAPACITY OF WATER, in gallons — *Rectangular/Square* — length (ft) × width (ft) × average depth (ft), then multiply by 6¼. *Round* — depth (ft) × diameter (ft) squared, then multiply by 4.9.

SURFACE AREA REQUIRED FOR COLDWATER FISH — 50sq cm for 10mm of fish, excluding tails.

POOL LINING — Size of sheeting required to line a pond:
max. length + 2 × depth = *length* of lining required
max. width + 2 × depth = *width* of lining required

1 pint = 0.57 litres
1 gallon = 4.55 litres
1 litre = .22 gallon
1 pound = .45kg
1 kilo = 2.2 pounds
1 gallon water = 10lb approximately

Recommended Reading

From the wide range of books about coldwater fish and related topics, I can thoroughly recommend the following. Despite the fact that some are now out of print, the fundamental arguments which underlie the whole art have not changed radically over the years, hence even the oldest still take places of honour on the bookshelf of the discriminating aquarist. Those marked with an asterisk *(*)* may be regarded as classics in their own right.

The Observer's Book of Freshwater Fishes of the British Isles —
A. Lawrence Wells — Warne
★*The Goldfish* — Hervey and Hems — Faber
Koi — Rose and Evans — Petfish
Goldfish — Anthony Evans — Foyles
★*Freshwater Fishes of the World* — Günther Sterba — Studio Vista
Goldfish Guide — Yoshiichi Matsui — Pet Library
★*Aquarium Plants* — de Wit — Blandford
The Water Garden — H.L.V. Fletcher — John Lehmann
Water Gardens — Frances Perry — Penguin
★*The Book of the Garden Pond* — Hervey and Hems — Faber
The Garden Pool — Frances Perry — Collingridge
A Manual of Aquarium Plants — Colin Roe — Shirley Aquatics
The Observer's Book of Pond Life — John Clegg — Warne
Aquariums — Anthony Evans — Foyles
Coldwater Fishkeeping — A. Boarder — Buckley Press
Fancy Goldfish Culture — F.W. Orme — Saiga Publishing Co.

The undermentioned monthly fishkeeping journals will enable you to keep in touch with current trends and techniques:

The Aquarist and Pondkeeper — Buckley Press, Brentford, Middlesex.
Practical Fishkeeping — EMAP, Peterborough.

The Goldfish Society of Great Britain *Show Standards* booklet will be of great interest to intending specialists in fancy goldfish, and may be obtained from the offices of The Aquarist and Pondkeeper.

Index